The Practical Guide to a Rapid Start-up

Launch Your Business in 20 Proven Steps

Melissa Visconti Moreno

Waterfront Press | 2259 Clear Lake Drive | Santa Maria, CA 93455

Subject Matter Expert
Jon Anton, D.Sc.

Cover & Book Design | Layout & Production
Mandy Schuldt, MS Graphic

Editor
Kimberly Nicoletti, M.A.

Research Associate
Robert Schuldt, B.B.A

Copyright ©2013 Melissa Visconti Moreno

Printed in the United States of America

All Rights Reserved. No part of this book
may be used or reproduced in any manner
without the written permission
from the Waterfront Press.

First printing — October 2013
Reprinted with minor corrections—January 20144
Third printing — August 2015

Author Acknowledgements

This book is dedicated to every person with a commitment and passion to act on an idea and launch a business.

"Plants always remain small under a big tree."
– Swami Vivekenanda

Thanks to Jon Anton, for without him, this book would not have been written. To Mark Kram for his loving suggestions and intellect. To Bonnie Chavez for his unwavering support of the activities at the Scheinfeld Center for Entrepreneurship & Innovation. To Santa Barbara City College for making a difference in the lives of student entrepreneurs.

Contents

Step 1
Brainstorm Ideas   1

   Failure Is a Good Teacher
   Ideas Are a Dime a Dozen
   Share Ideas in a Relaxed Environment
   Promote Positive Feedback
   Create a Big List and Casually Vote

Step 2
Check Feasibility   9

   Create a List of the Top 10 Ideas
   Use the Internet to Find the Same Thing
   Look for Ideas that Appeal to Local Consumers
   Consider Scalability
   Can You Make a Prototype within Weeks?
   Can You Launch for Under $10,000?
   Will A Lot of People Likely Buy It?
   Select the Top-Rated Ideas to Pursue Further
   Case Study: Cuppow

Step 3
Build Your Team   23

   Self Analysis of Skill Sets
   Build a Team Based on Complementary Skill Sets
   Self-Assessment of Personality Type
   Team Formation
   Match a Product to the Team
   Address Ownership of Your New Venture
   Plan on Things Going Wrong
   The Importance of a Positive Attitude

Step 4
Recruit Mentors　　　　　　　　　　　　　　35
Choosing Mr. (or Mrs.) Right
Case Study: FlashPals

Step 5
Study the Industry　　　　　　　　　　　　43
Find Key Statistics about Your Industry
Why Industry Information Is Important
Possible Delimiters

Step 6
Target Your Market　　　　　　　　　　　　51
How to Define Your Target Customer
Talk to Your Customers
Ask More Questions about Your Customers
Consider Geography and Seasonality
Is This a Single Purchase Product?
Case Study: Reddit

Step 7
Contact Customers　　　　　　　　　　　　61
Gather Informal Feedback from Customers
Create a More Formal Survey Based on Informal Feedback
To Proceed or Not to Proceed? That Is the Question!

Step 8
Protect Your Ideas　　　　　　　　　　　　69
Two Simple Practices
Three Main Concerns
Trademark/Service Mark
Copyright
Patent
Non-Disclosure Agreements

Step 9
Analyze the Competition   79

- Admit You Have Competitors
- View Your Product Objectively
- Revisit Your Industry Analysis

Step 10
Differentiate   87

- Unique Operating Characteristics
- Unique Marketing Platforms
- Unique Distribution or Sales Strategies
- Case Study: FlightCar

Step 11
Build Your Prototype   95

- Essential Aspects to Consider in Creating an Initial Prototype
- Use Cheap, Accessible Materials
- Spend Less Than $300
- Feeling Like It's Obsolete Already?

Step 12
Evolve Your Prototype   101

- Take Stock & Consider Scrapping Your Idea, Again
- Focus
- Conduct Another Round of Customer Interviews
- Capture Testimonials

Step 13
Sell Prototypes   109

- Why Sell Now?
- How to Sell
- Your Purpose Is to Get Early Fans of Your Product

Step 14
Know the Numbers — 115
    Profit & Loss
    Balance Sheet
    Break-Even Analysis
    Cash Flow Analysis

Step 15
Layout Marketing — 123
    Marketing Tools
    Be Consistent
    Social Media
    Build Your Own Temporary Website
    Traditional Advertising & Networking
    Placement

Step 16
Outline Operations — 131
    Point of Sales (POS) Systems
    Bookkeeping & Payroll Services
    Manufacturing

Step 17
Chart Distribution — 139
    Plan for a Sales Team
    Customer Service
    Payment Terms
    Distribution
    Case Study: iCracked

Step 18
Consider Investment   147

    What You Want in an Investor
    What an Investor Wants in You
    Angel Investors
    Investment Rounds
    Venture Capital

Step 19
Pitch, Pitch, Pitch   157

    How to Deliver Great Pitches
    Slide Deck & Props
    Appearance and Body Language
    Prepare Answers to Tough Questions
    Connect with Judges
    Case Study: Big Fish

Step 20
Plan the Exit   167

    Acquisition
    Licensing
    Earn-Out

Extras
More Reviews   175
Student Testimonials   179
Appendices   199
Biographies   211

Legal Disclaimer: We have attached sample legal agreements to be used for reference purposes only. We do not recommend any legal form in this book for your use, and these forms are not offered as legal advice. We do not give legal advice in this book; it is up to you to seek appropriate legal advising with a lawyer in your state.

Introduction

In an economic environment where 50% of college graduates are working in jobs that don't require an education at all [1], entrepreneurship becomes a very attractive choice for millenials. Young people need to consider creating their own jobs, and this book introduces you to a tried and true method for launching your own business in a short period of time. You can't make money while sitting in the classroom. We have proven that students can create their own business and start selling in a single semester, and have fun doing it.

This book is a step-by-step guide to a rapid launch of a product or service[2] in about 4 months. It is written for entrepreneurs interested in learning the ropes by testing a small idea before jumping into the big shark tank. The lessons you learn with this first attempt will serve your next, bigger endeavor in ways you cannot imagine. You can also use this book to help you prepare for pitch competitions, investor pitches, or the Startup Weekend experience. This book is also written for educators and facilitators who teach in entrepreneurship programs, conduct workshops, host Startup Weekends, or have college labs focused on the rapid launch of a product or service in a limited timeframe.

If you are an entrepreneur with an existing idea, please skip ahead to step 2 or 3 — or pick and choose steps as you feel they relate to you. There are no hard and fast rules about how you tackle this book. We are simply attempting to show you the proven steps we have shared with our

---

1 *The Nation's Recent College Graduates Face Significant Labor Market Problems*, (2010) Andrew Sum, Professor of Economics at Northeastern University.

2 Throughout this book, we will refer to a "product or service" simply as a "product." All concepts presented equally apply to a service, and where they deviate, we will clarify.

students — steps that have taken our students from nothing to success. You can approach this book from an entrepreneur standpoint as a DIY. And, if you are thinking about pitching at a local Startup Weekend, our steps can help you prepare for what's in store for the next 54 hours.

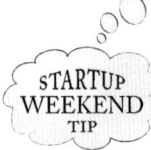

Startup Weekend Disclaimer: In each step heading, we give "Startup Weekend Tips." These tips are in no way endorsed by the Startup Weekend organization. These tips are based solely on our knowledge of working everyday with new entrepreneurs. The usefulness of the tips are based on our observations from attending Startup Weekend events that we think might or could be helpful to attendees, mentors, participants or facilitators. We encourage all entrepreneurs to check out Startup Weekend events in your area. It is an opportunity to pitch a concept, and as we say in step 19, pitch as often as possible in as many venues as you can.

On the other hand, if you are an educator or facilitator, your program can be customized according to need, and this guide can be used in two ways: It can be adopted as the complete curriculum of the program or simply drawn from to help develop a customized program. The activities in this book take 40 to 60 hours to complete. We have built 20 steps (or modules), each of which can be taught in up to a 3-hour timeframe (60 hours total). It contains 20 additional hours of activities (i.e., 4 hours for industry research, 8 hours for customer validation activities, 4 hours of competitive research, 4 hours of operations research, and 4 hours in distribution planning), which can and should be completed outside the lab as homework or research.

Throughout the book, we occasionally highlight an existing company with founders who are exemplary of the start-up principles we promote.

x   The Practical Guide to a Rapid Start-up

Comic strips: In each step you will see a comic strip playfully demonstrating interaction between the key personalities necessary for a team: the Driver (leader, visionary, deadline-setter), the Expressive (sales person, extrovert, pitcher), the Amiable (problem solver, people person, has feelings), and the Analytic (technical expertise, analyst, numbers person). We conclude that every entrepreneur needs help, and finding the right balance of personalities and skill sets on your team is critical to your success. Each role is significant and equally important.

ANALYTIC   DRIVER   AMIABLE   EXPRESSIVE

This book is an outcropping of our own personal experiences in building businesses, which we extensively tested for 2 years at the Scheinfeld Center for Entrepreneurship & Innovation at Santa Barbara City College. We formulated a program called Enterprise Launch™ to help students quickly launch products or services in a single semester. In an age when attention spans are diminishing by such rapid access to information, entrepreneurs have less patience for traditional classroom approaches. We know, because when we launched this program on campus, we sparked exceptional interest by students. We had more than 50 students attend our first orientation. In the community college world, students willing to commit 3 hours a week for a non-credit experience proved we were tapping into unprecedented enthusiasm and a thirst for innovation and creativity. Entrepreneurs want the practical version of education — anything that gives them a leg up, helps them mitigate the risks associated with starting a new business, and gives them essential tools and information they need to actually launch a business — rapidly.

Our tools are designed to efficiently build a business and begin selling within 4 months. The businesses that generally result from this process tend to be small at first and possess potential scalability with a clear exit plan — perfect for Startup Weekenders. Our goal is to help you experience the process of becoming an entrepreneur with the least possible risk and lowest possible financial investment. One of the cornerstones of our philosophy is: crawl, walk, and then run. Your business might only last 1 year, but in that year you learn how to create something from nothing and make money while doing it. This process hopefully prepares you for your next, bigger idea. Let's be real. This book probably won't help you build an engineering based business where $5 million is invested up front for research and development. This book, however, does contain a proven formula for starting a small, yet scalable, business. The steps include: taking a realistic concept that utilizes your own (and your team's) existing skills, adding your own available resources, and creating a prototype and a plan for selling your product or service within a few months so that you start making money. A few examples of our funded success stories include Garden on Wheelz™ (a mobile, raised gardening bed for wheelchair-bound or older people to continue their love of gardening); Embrace™ (a double-layered sleeve worn under a cast or brace to prevent chafing and infection); and NAK™ (a sleek, compact nail accessory kit used as a branded promotional item ("swag") for company giveaways at tradeshows or for company gift-giving).

Our program works for our students, and we know it will work for you, too. With Startup Weekends cropping up all over the nation — where participants spend 54 hours in a long weekend developing products — this guide is the essential "go to" book for entrepreneurs.

 *Credit or Non-Credit? For the first 2 years (4 semesters), we offered this program as a non-credit student club. This had an interesting and unexpected outcome. Fifty students each semester, without fail, vied for a seat in the room. We had about 35 stay the course, showing up each week, for 13 weeks, ready to go. No credit. No grade. No reason to attend, other than the sheer curiosity of what might be possible. We are currently testing a credit program, and will let you know how a "for credit" offering changes the nature of the program. We are dead set on creating the same "playground" environment, no matter what.*

Brainstorm Ideas

Generating ideas for new products and services is an unstructured, creative process during which spontaneity should not only be tolerated, but also encouraged. In this step, we help increase the probability of a positive outcome. If you already have an idea or several ideas, skip ahead to next steps.

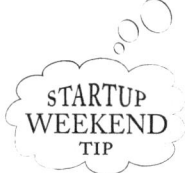

AT STARTUP WEEKENDS, ENTREPRENEURS COME PREPARED TO PITCH IDEAS AND USUALLY ONLY HAVE 1 MINUTE! THIS SEGMENT PROVIDES SOME PRE-WEEKEND EXERCISES TO HELP FORMULATE A SPECIFIC IDEA INTO A CONVINCING PITCH.

Failure Is a Good Teacher

Before we begin, we would like to address the concept of failure. Everyone's first fear in business is the fear of failure. We all know the miserable statistics on small business failure and the low chances for long-term sustainability. In general, only 1 in 100 start-up attempts actually make it. By contrast, according to our observations, entrepreneurs who fail on the first try and then pursue a new idea double their chances of succeeding. Failure is a good teacher.

We understand from personal experiences that failure is inevitable. But we also know that failure is a valuable learning experience. It teaches you what you did wrong and often demonstrates how sometimes external factors that you have no control over can delay or kill your business if you have no contingency plan. Some examples of tough-to-overcome external factors include nature, politics, the economy, our government, construction, and key partners going bankrupt. It's hard to anticipate everything, but failure teaches you to have a contingency plan.

This book shows you how to build a business in a very short period of time with a small idea, so you can start making money with very little cash outlay and minimal risk. Through that process, you learn more than you ever thought possible. We would rather you crash and burn on a small idea than on the big one that costs $5 million to start.

Here is a list of five key reasons start-ups can fail:
1. You end up hating what you are doing, so you give up.
2. You didn't plan properly and didn't get to know your numbers (so you ran out of cash or were undercapitalized).
3. You failed to surround yourself with a winning team of partners, employees, and mentors.
4. Any number of unanticipated and uncontrolled external factors affected your ability to move ahead, and you did not have a contingency plan.
5. You built a business for you (as opposed to "for your customers"), and it forever depends on you.

Take a look at the photo on the book cover. This was taken in 1901 of the Wright Brothers' attempting flight near Kitty Hawk Beach in North Carolina. The results of this attempt in 1901 (and others before and after) were discouraging. After a year's attempts at flight, Wilbur Wright wrote: "When we left Kitty Hawk at the end of 1901, we doubted that we would ever resume our experiments. Although we had broken the record for distance in gliding... when we looked at the time and money which we had expended, and considered the progress made and the distance yet to go, we considered our experiments a failure.

At this time I made the prediction that men would sometime fly, but that it would not be within our lifetime." (Emphasis added.) Wilbur was very discouraged and felt they had failed. In fact, this quote morphed over the years to read, "Not within a thousand years would man ever fly." The Wright Brothers conquered flight 2 years later.

Ideas Are a Dime a Dozen

Every idea is good, or even great. Entrepreneurs naturally have many ideas. But if you don't know how to execute your ideas to creaate a successful business, your ideas don't matter.

If you are starting this book with several ideas already, skip to the next steps and test your ideas for feasibility for a rapid launch.

This step helps you derive new ideas in a creative environment, with an eye toward a rapid start-up. This step is especially helpful to facilitators running a group session or program. If you are an entrepreneur, we suggest you gather a group of friends to run a brainstorming session of your own. Throw a brainstorming dinner party. The results will surprise you.

Jump right into brainstorming and practice pitching. It sets a pace and tone that continues throughout a program. And, not surprisingly, it's one of the most exciting and contagious activities, which gets participants fired up and ready to pitch. The use of activities and tools revs up creative juices and helps establish somewhat of a free-for-all environment. It is absolutely necessary to set the tone from the outset that this is a casual environment, or "playground," where there are no bad ideas. During this early program stage, emphasize the quantity of ideas, rather than quality. There will be plenty of time for analysis of quality concepts and positive critiquing later. This initial part of the program is designed to get everyone comfortable pitching concepts and sharing ideas, over and over again. As you move through numerous ideas, you start to see a pattern develop for those that best qualify for a rapid launch.

Create a Confidential Zone: Whenever you gather a group of potential entrepreneurs or inventors together to share ideas, consider how to protect those ideas. Brainstorming sessions will fail if comfort and confidentiality are not established from the outset. Having everyone sign Non-Disclosure Agreements (NDA) has proven effective with our students. (See Appendix D for a sample NDA). An NDA helps to create a sacred confidential zone at the first meeting. You need to establish a confidential environment so that everyone can share freely without fearing that ideas will be stolen. If you are an educator or facilitator, please seek legal advice prior to the initial session to nail down your NDA. Monitor the comings and goings of students and participants carefully. Late arrivals, mentors, advisors, and visitors must sign an NDA before entering the confidential zone.

Share Ideas in a Relaxed Environment

First, establish a relaxed, open, and sharing environment, in order to encourage all participants to "free flow" their ideas, no matter how stupid or silly they might seem or feel at the time. This is not the time to be shy or insecure. Some of the best ideas emerge from a spontaneous outburst during a "free-flow" session.

If you are the one leading the group, set the ground rules to completely avoid negative commentary. Comments like the following (and other showstoppers) should be avoided: "That will never work," or "I have seen that before." Group creativity tends to fall flat when members of the group see someone's idea trashed. So bite your tongue and let all ideas enter the arena. Do not allow others to criticize anyone's idea (not yet). This must remain a positive exercise for the purpose of building a trusting and comfortable environment.

Ways to loosen people up and stimulate ideas include: moving desks or furniture around, walking around or dancing, listening to music for a couple minutes, and watching a 2-minute slideshow of inspirational images (of nature, people, phenomenon, etc.).

You can also engage in preliminary, short, icebreaker exercises, such as:
- Speed networking: Walk around, greet one person, and then share your "number one" passion with each other in 60 seconds. When the 1-minute timer goes off, switch partners.
- Pass a box around, and ask every participant to anonymously write his or her biggest fear on a slip of paper and place it into the box. Randomly pull fears out, and openly discuss them. You will hear "fear of failure" often and, as a group, you can use this as an opportunity to discuss how failure is a steppingstone to an entrepreneur's success.

Then begin the process of idea sharing by asking participants to either share new ideas or talk about ones they have been thinking about for a while. Encourage crazy or silly ideas, related to anything. A playful mind is always a creative mind. Continue to elicit thoughts from participants until they run dry of new ideas. You'll notice how natural peer pressure helps each participant up the ante and add one better idea than the previously volunteered idea.

Promote Positive Feedback

As the session unfolds, provide positive feedback for all ideas, regardless of how unrealistic they may seem at the time. Participants should use simple words of encouragement, like "great idea." Also include supportive body language, such as smiling and applauding.

At this point, control and minimize questions about "how it would work," and instead focus on understanding the idea, as nebulous as it may sound. We tend to naturally poo-poo ideas because of thoughts like, "This won't work!" "How will you ever manufacture it?" "No one will buy that!" Keep those comments at bay and know that details like these are not important at this stage. Sticking with "high level" concepts is key. Open-ended questions can spark even more discussion. Try questions, such as:
- Does this idea help you personally?
- Would this idea help a group or class of people?
- Does this idea fix something that is missing in our world?

- Does this idea make something in our world better?
- Does this idea feel good?

Remember: Try not to judge new ideas immediately. Instead, support the process of exploring and developing ideas, because a later session will allow time for analyzing ideas by conducting a preliminary feasibility check.

In this creative phase, remain mostly on an emotional level, assuming a positive business outcome, even though your tendency may be to move too quickly to the rational level and begin tearing ideas apart. (Note to group leaders: Be sure to direct all participants to remain on the creative and supportive level.)

Create a Big List and Casually Vote

As you move through the brainstorming session, create a list of the many ideas shared using a whiteboard, chalkboard, walls or an easel. You can post ideas all around the room using paper and tape. You want to fill the room with ideas!

At the end of the session, you can opt to purge ideas with a casual vote. Or, you might create a friendly competition by rewarding the person with the most unique ideas once the creative session ends. Or, you can use Post-its or painter's tape and have each participant place a vote on the top three "perceived" best ideas at the end. The ideas with the most Post-its win... for now.

Check Feasibility

Once you have generated ideas, the process becomes much more structured and analytical. This step describes a method for a preliminary measure of a concept's potential feasibility and marketability. Thus begins the selection process.

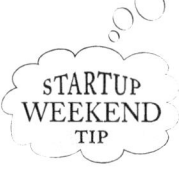

THIS SEGMENT PROVIDES VALUABLE QUESTIONS TO THINK ABOUT AS AN ATTENDEE/VOTER DURING THE "PITCHFIRE" AND VOTING PHASE.

By now, you should have a list of about 20 ideas that seem worth looking into a little further. This is where we begin vetting the concepts for potential success in the weeks ahead. Ideally, you want to pare the concepts down to your top 10. Also during this process, you might notice that teams begin to organically form. People become naturally attracted to certain ideas and gravitate toward each other. Allow it to happen.

Create a List of the Top 10 Ideas

As you scan the list of ideas from the brainstorming sessions, look for product or service opportunities. Ask these questions:

1. Does your product idea solve an existing "pain" for the customer?
   Focus on situations where people have expressed their pains by telling you, "If only this product had _____, it would be so much easier to use." Reflect on your own experiences where you have expressed a need for something that doesn't exist. These feelings are valid and lead to great ideas! Don't second-guess the value by thinking only you need it — if *you* need it, most likely others need it too.

   Bring physical examples of existing products (include some of which are "failures" from the "As Seen on TV" store, or from the Dollar Store). Instruct your group to look at these existing products, and then ask team members to guess what pain each product solved. Ask them to consider whether or not the product is successful and why.

   You might bring in a half dozen different types of wine bottle openers and discuss how they differ and how each addresses a different pain point.

2. Does your product idea make customers "feel good"?
   Shoppers are now buying re-usable cloth bags for grocery shopping. It certainly feels good to help protect the environment. (Note: The reusable bags also solve a pain — reducing pollution and saving animals. Your product can certainly both feel good and solve a pain.)

   For this session, try to think of those areas where there are feel-good possibilities, for instance: saving water, composting fruit and vegetable scraps, and protecting your skin from the sun's ultraviolet rays (the latter also solves a pain — preventing skin cancer).

   Remember, classic "feel-good" products are luxury items — namely, those that society doesn't necessarily need to survive, such as:

- scented lotion,
- perfume,
- fashion-forward related products (like fancy shoes and designer clothing), and
- jewelry.

3. Can you make a case that your product idea both feels good and solves a pain?

    Obviously, the best products achieve both: They provide relief from pain, and it feels good to buy and use them.

    An example might be a scented candle: It brings light to the darkness (a potential pain), and it emanates a great smell (a potential feel-good feature).

 *We also highly recommend the ideation and feasibility worksheets located in the DIY Innovation Toolkit at www.theinnographer.com. These tools help you choose ideas that have the most potential for success: those with concurrent high impact and high feasibility.*

Use the Internet to Find the Same Thing

Once you've answered the above questions, do a thorough Internet search early to assess how unique your idea is.

First, determine whether or not your exact idea (or something very close) already exists. The following is an anecdotal example of something that already existed: One team came up with an idea called "The Bucket List." They pitched creating a website (social network) for older folks looking for adventure as they aged so that participants could check off everything they have always wanted to do. It was a great idea! But, a website with this unique name already existed, offering that very same service. The team members did not do their research until after they had

Check Feasibility

put a lot of time and energy into developing the idea. They researched about 3 weeks into their efforts, to their grave disappointment.

Researching early is critical to ensure you don't waste your time. Do a quick Google search to assess the broad picture of what is out there. If you find something too similar, tweak your idea to differentiate it from what already exists by changing or adding features, or discard it and start all over. Sometimes the decision to discard an idea is harder than it seems. Learning that an identical product exists later in the game is sometimes unavoidable. Perhaps another company just launched the product and the information became available after you began working on your idea. In this case, seriously consider scrapping your idea. The other manufacturer probably has a significant head start, and perhaps the company is doing a great job. Don't be married to your idea, just because you thought of it. The goal is to land on a product idea or improvement that hasn't already been done, or that you can easily do better.

If your product seems as though it varies enough, keep searching to find out if something similar exists. Begin to look for similarities in form and function. Accept the fact that it is nearly impossible to come up with an idea that no one has ever envisioned. However, slight improvements, and added features, can help you redefine what the customer wants and is willing to buy. When Yvon Chouinard (founder of Patagonia) visited the Scheinfeld Center, an overzealous student came up to the mic during the Q&A and asked if he could have a meeting with Yvon to pitch this great idea he had! Yvon took the wind out of his sails rather quickly. Yvon said that he could guarantee this student's idea had already been thought of, considered, and is being worked on, or had been discarded for a good reason — without even hearing his idea! Yvon's point is well taken. Your idea is likely already out there. The question is whether anyone acted on it and is doing it really well.

If something similar exists, notice the differences in price and target market segment. For instance, high-performance kayaks were a hit with thrill-seekers in whitewater rivers. Then someone invented the "sit-on-top" kayak for the leisure-minded outdoor person, and a new target market was defined, but a kayak is still a kayak.

Also assess the amount of overlap your idea has with an existing product, and acknowledge the fact that seldom will another product be exactly like yours. This is why new products are often invented by a customer who is using the current version, which is "lacking" something. For example, a kayaker once noted how fun it would be to fish from a kayak. But, there was no way to hold the fishing pole in place on the kayak. Because of this "lacking" feeling, the person involved invented a fishing pole holder, which bolts to the deck of the kayak, and is now very popular with kayakers who want to fish from their boats. It is that simple to create a whole new concept from something that already exists — by adding a feature that appeals to a potentially large targeted market segment.

Finally, determine whether or not your idea possesses enough unique features to still compete with an existing, but similar, product.

Once you discover your idea is not as original as you thought, it is sometimes disappointing. However, your enthusiasm regenerates after you refine your idea and it becomes more potentially viable. Begin to analyze its viability, and ask how your product truly differs.

For starters, think about how your product is better. Better can be defined in many ways, like cheaper, more functional, lighter, more durable, and much more.

You can also weigh how your product is not as good. It is always tough for inventors to be honest about their products. But, just realize, the best critique about your product should come from target customers. If you don't recognize your product's weak points, just ask a potential customer, and you'll get an "earful." (We will discuss target market and customer validation techniques, as well as protecting your idea as you take it out into the market, in upcoming steps.)

Look for Ideas that Appeal to Local Consumers

Now it's time to take a preliminary look at whether or not your product targets local customers.

If you are going to be successful with a "rapid" start-up, we strongly recommend starting with locally accessible customers. Ideally, you will have face-to-face access with real, potential customers with whom you can immediately begin interacting. The benefit is: You are likely more familiar with and better understand your geographic location, the culture and attitudes of the people, and general likes and dislikes of your local population, as opposed to a national demographic. We also believe that starting small and proving your concept locally is a decided advantage for a low-budget launch. The biggest challenge for any company launch is having enough money. The vast majority of start-ups crash from lack of funding.

Start-ups also fail due to lack of customer input from the very beginning. It is important to consult your customers from the outset. Getting customers involved in your new product is essential and saves both money and time in the long run. Design your product for and with your customers, not in a vacuum.

Consider Scalability

For the best chance of success, your product should be potentially scalable. There are many definitions of scalable. Some experts and investors define it as the potential to grow sales to the hundreds of millions. For purposes of a rapid start-up, we define scalable as the ability to grow the business into a franchise, or to a point where you are able to "make money while you are sleeping," as Paul Ofalea would say. In other words, can you grow it enough so you can comfortably afford to hire people to do the work you were doing to get the business started, so the business no longer depends only on your time and skills to get the job done? This is a critical point worth emphasizing. You cannot scale your business when you are the only one that knows how to run it. In addition, it may be your personal purpose to own a business so that you can afford a certain amount of leisure living. How can you ever take a surf trip around the world if your business depends on you every minute?

Can You Make a Prototype within Weeks?

It's also important to be able to create an initial prototype within weeks, because we are working on a rapid start-up. That means you must create something to show potential customers quickly. An important question to consider is whether or not you can make this prototype yourself. We will discuss prototyping in detail in a later step, however, we must make a preliminary assessment as to whether you can pull off a rough demonstration, drawing, webpage, or some physical manifestation of the product in the next 4 weeks. It also helps if you can make the prototype yourself.

Here are what some students have done in the past:
- one of our students used a torch in his bedroom (not recommended) to solder metal parts to mock up a prototype and brought it to class;
- another student stole parts from his roommates' computer speakers (again, not recommended) to make his prototype;
- one student used his grandfather's lathe to make a prototype;
- other students used CAD drawings to demonstrate their products; and
- some students used a 3D printer to make molds for their prototypes.

You will need to consider whether or not you have the particular skill or ability to pull off a rough demonstration within a few weeks to show how your product works.

Unless you have plenty of your own "seed" money (seldom the case in your first start-up), it is better if your product is something you can build yourself. This ability allows you to test the market without having to rely on a manufacturing company to build your prototype product.

Can You Launch for Under $10,000?

In addition, this product should be something you can launch for less than $10,000. When you take your first start-up journey, attracting

capital from "angel" investors is very difficult, so therefore, if you're asking for $10,000 or less, your chance of attaining the needed sponsorship is greater.

At this stage, we also advise avoiding products that are heavily regulated with potential barriers to entry, such as ingestible products. Steer clear of products like food and medicinal products. Food products require governmental approval and are highly regulated. Medicinal products require all kinds of expensive studies and research, and the regulations can stifle a small company. Products for the skin are probably okay, but beware of the regulations in this industry and the restrictions on claims. Remember: Advertising claims must be totally verifiable, otherwise, you risk litigation. Any legal problems for a start-up can be a major survival risk.

Will A Lot of People Likely Buy It?

Once you've gone through a checklist for these potential delimiters, ask yourself if this is a product you would really buy. The best products are designed around real customers. If you can find one of those early "evangelist" customers, the likelihood that the product comes out perfect is enhanced.

In summary, here is a winning strategy for choosing the best products for a rapid start-up:
- It encourages a local launch
- Meets a local need
- Is cheap to make and run with
- Is potentially scalable nationally, or even globally.

Select the Top-Rated Ideas to Pursue Further

Once you have gone through this feasibility check for each idea, you should probably be able to naturally discard about half of the 20 ideas you started with. Run through the checklist for each idea, and decide which ideas hold up against the assessment.

Use the preliminary feasibility checklist, which we presented in an easy to follow grid format. Use this to check each idea.

NAME OF IDEA:	YES	NO
Does your product solve an existing pain?		
Does your product make customers feel good?		
Does your idea already exist?		
Does something similar exist?		
Does your idea have unique features/benefits?		
Does your product target local and accessible customers?		
Is your product scalable?		
Can you make a prototype in the next 4 weeks?		
Is this a product you would buy?		
Are their potential major barriers to entry (i.e. FDA regs)?		
Is this a product that costs less than $10,000 for an initial launch?		

Table 1. Feasibility Checklist

If, after you have conducted the analysis and the top 10 are not clearly apparent, participants may "weigh" each product on a 1 to 3 rating scale, where 1 = must have, 2 = nice to have, and finally, 3 = discard from the list.

You will find Notes pages like this one strewn throughout the book for your convenience to jot down your inspirations or ideas.

NOTES

(Left to right) Greg Ralich, Operations Manager, Joshua Resnikoff, and Aaron Panone

The Cuppow founders set the example for the principles shared in this book. They started their company with less than $5,000, created prototypes, and bootstrapped to produce record sales in a single year.

The Founders

Aaron Panone received a dual-discipline BS in Electrical and Mechanical Engineering from Wentworth Institute of Technology, thereafter becoming a specialist in mechanical design and creative solutions, and ultimately product development. Initially, Cuppow was a side project for Aaron that took on a life of its own. Currently, as a part-time co-CEO and creative director at Cuppow, he continues to pursue his interests in design, and work with select clients.

Mission Statement > Cuppow is an American company that grew out of a need to develop everyday products that would help decrease our own eco-footprint. Our flagship Cuppow product - the original drinking lid adaptor for mason jars - allows people to up-cycle an everyday item into an eco-friendly travel mug, and we bring this same intention into all of our products by designing for utility and simplicity. Our products utilize BPA and phthalate free food-grade recycled plastic as part of our ongoing commitment to divert as much needless waste as possible from the landfill.

We believe that all responsible businesses should be reinvesting in their communities, so we are proud to commit 5% of profits toward supporting other like-minded organizations and domestic charities that focus on engaging people on environmental stewardship, recycling, and social awareness.

Company Growth > With an initial investment of $3200, we were able to design and purchase 500 pieces, and develop a limited online infrastructure for e-commerce. Relying almost exclusively on social media and peer-to-peer marketing strategies, we've been able to bootstrap our company to the point of selling over 140,000 units in our first year alone. Despite being approached by multiple venture capitalists, we have declined investment and opted to minimize our exposure and debt. Although this limited the EOY payouts, it allowed us to grow along our vision, retain control of all our processes, and stay true to our core values.

Business Model > The Cuppow jar drinking lid and the BNTO jar lunchbox are designed to turn the all-American mason jar into a useful and environmentally-friendly travel mug or lunchbox. Both the Cuppow and BNTO are made in the USA from 100 percent recycled and recyclable food-safe plastic that's BPA, BPS and phthalate-free, so they're safe for the whole family.

3

Build Your Team

Once you have narrowed down the selection to a list of top 10 ideas that have potential in the marketplace, it is time to build an effective founding team around each idea. In this step, we share effective exercises for determining complementary skills and personalities to improve your success in bringing the product to market with your team.

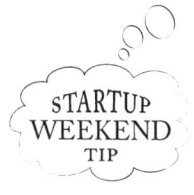

> **STARTUP WEEKEND TIP**
>
> FORMING TEAMS AT THE OUTSET IS PART OF THE STARTUP WEEKEND CULTURE. YOUR RAPID-FIRE PITCH INCLUDES ASKING FOR SKILLS YOU REALLY NEED THAT COMPLEMENT YOUR OWN. GIVE SOME SERIOUS ADVANCE CONSIDERATION TO WHAT SKILLS YOU REALLY NEED TO MAKE YOUR IDEA HAPPEN.

Forming a working team is essential to being successful in such a short period of time. You can't do everything by yourself! Paul Orfalea (founder of Kinko's) once told the Scheinfeld Center that he considered his disabilities (dyslexia and ADHD) a gift because they forced him to reach out and team up with people who had skills he didn't have. He knew he would never be successful without a team and tells us no one can be successful alone. We agree.

Self Analysis of Skill Sets

In order to know where you fit into your team, it's essential to complete a self-assessment of both skills and personality. First, using the Matrix of Skills in Appendix A, complete each square to identify your own strengths, weaknesses, opportunities and threats. (It is a personal SWOT analysis). When you share this information with your potential team, it becomes clear how to construct a team based on complementary skills. This matrix highlights your strengths, allows you to assess others' strengths and match up with team members who demonstrate different strengths than you, to help shore up your weaknesses.

Build a Team Based on Complementary Skill Sets

When you begin selecting teams, find partners who have complementary skill sets, and, in most cases, avoid selecting partners with the same skill sets. Because there are many useful skills needed when starting a company, it is more productive to select partners who are additive to your skill set, not duplicative. Think of your company as a team with players who possess different talents and play various positions. For example, people who run very fast will probably not play in the line in football. Instead, they will be wide receivers, or running backs. In business, we have seen teams consisting of one creative person, one natural public speaker, one shy and technical person, and one high achiever.

Seldom do you possess all the skills that are needed to be successful, hence the need for complementary partners. Often, people naturally realize the skills they lack or are clear on the responsibilities they don't want. For example, you may abhor the thought of being responsible for the accounting function, but others declare they are great with numbers and find the challenge of accounting fun. You must find the right mix of skillful people to succeed, and the Matrix of Skills will help you determine that mix.

Self-Assessment of Personality Type

Next, take the Personality Self-Assessment in Appendix B, page 1. Circle all the traits that apply to you, and calculate your personality type and career interests in steps 1 and 2. Then total both sections to determine your main and secondary personality types.

This is a proven qualitative test, so don't circle a trait unless you can verify you definitely have it. This self-assessment effort is meant to be tough. You want to be as honest as you can be, so leave your ego at the door. Be realistic about your traits — claim the characteristics you have, not those you *want* to have. For instance, if you think you're a driver, ask yourself if you have held any leadership positions. Have you been a club president or captain of a sports team? If you want to be a leader but have never filled any leadership roles, steer clear from claiming it as one of your strong points.

All personality types are equally important, so don't try to be something you're not really comfortable being just because you think you will appear more important and be placed in a "higher" position. All personalities on the team hold the same value.

After each person on your team conducts a personality analysis, it will become clear where each person fits in. The Personality Self-Assessment will help each member determine his or her key business personal type. This step is critical to creating a successful business team. The four personalities, and their descriptions, are:

1. **Driver:** This is the leader-type person who has vision and direction, likes to create "to do" lists, set goals and deadlines, and achieves results. He or she usually takes the president or CEO position of the company. This is a very key position. Assign this team position only after much analysis and discussion.
2. **Expressive:** This is the person who has a natural ability to articulate ideas and get others to buy-in. He or she typically takes the sales role in the company. This will also be your "pitch" person. Typically, this person is charismatic, likes taking action, and is lively, animated, optimistic, and full of boundless energy. It is often very easy to identify this person. Don't be fooled into

making this person the president, as this personality type often needs to be closely directed for the best results.

3. **Amiable:** This is the person who is most interested in everyone "getting along," is tuned into people's feelings, and intuitively understands boundaries. He or she typically works in human resources and mediates issues or problems. Don't underestimate the importance of this person. Having a team that works well together is often the result of the feeling and sensitivity of the amiable team member.

4. **Analytic:** This is the technical "numbers person" who thrives on solving product problems and accounting for the results. He or she usually likes math and science courses and holds an accounting role in the company as Controller or CFO, or sometimes leads the engineering department. An analytic can also be the programmer or developer on your team.

Figure 3-1. The Four Personality Types

If, after completing the assessment, you are still a little unsure about your own dominant business personality type, team up with other people of your type for an open discussion. Ask questions like, "Do you all have similar skills and likes? What are the dominant traits in the group?" After this discussion with others in your category, you will be more certain as to whether you belong in the group.

Remember: All four of the above personalities are absolutely necessary for success. Be critical in assessing who best fits each personality. You will find you fit into one or more types, but we ask that you determine your *dominant* type based on your own assessment. Don't take this responsibility lightly. Teaming up with the wrong personality type jeopardizes the organization and potentially causes team members to fail to meet their goals. Worse yet, negative infighting occurs, and valuable time and energy will be lost. In the worst-case scenario, the team implodes, and the only out is a corporate divorce, resulting in a false start, wasted time, and sometimes outright failure.

Take a look at page 2 of Appendix B: The Entrepreneur Self-Evaluation. This test measures whether you have the right mix of characteristics common to entrepreneurs. If you take this test, you can get a sense of your likelihood of success as an entrepreneur in terms of you possessing the right combination of entrepreneurial traits. On a scale of 1 to 10, rate your strength of this trait, then multiply your score across the row using the designated weight score to determine your final score for that trait. For example, if you feel you are a 7 in possessing courage, multiply 7 by the weight score of 6 and your total for trait number 3 (Courageous) is 42. Continue the calculations for each trait and determine your total and see where you stand in terms of your likelihood for success. This is a benchmarking tool to assess where you are today, and look at the traits you might need to develop for a more successful future.

Team Formation

Now that you have determined your skill-set and dominant personality, it's time to form a team. If you are leading a class, you can conduct an exercise, and group together personality types and assign numbers (Driver = 1, Expressive = 2, Amiable = 3, Analytic = 4) to help others recognize who they need on their team. Also, beware of forming a team with more than one driver personality. When new teams form with more than one driver, the situation can deteriorate quickly, and no one knows who is in charge. The best teams have a clear leader who effectively sets a direction and vision and helps lead the effort in establishing goals and milestones.

WE NEED TO BUILD A STRONG TEAM. BUT, WE'RE ON A TIGHT SCHEDULE. WHO WILL HELP ME?
WHO WOULD BE HAPPY DOING WHAT TO HELP?

IF YOU GIVE ME THE FACTS, I'LL WORK UP THE NUMBERS
LET'S TALK MORE ABOUT IT!

Match a Product to the Team

Now it's time to claim the product that matches the team's interests and skills. You have 10 to 12 products and therefore need 10 to 12 teams (one for each concept). There is a bit of an organic process here that cannot necessarily be controlled. You might wait and see what happens naturally in terms of teams aligning with business ideas. Sometimes the visionary of the concept becomes the team leader (driver) and picks his or her mates to develop his/her own concept. Usually visionaries are emotionally attached to their own idea. However, we have often seen leaders pair with someone else's idea — they scrap their own in search of a better, potentially more successful idea. We strongly encourage concept choice be driven by the potential for success rather than driven by emotional attachment. There are no hard-and-fast rules here, but whoever emerges as a leader may be the best person to choose the remainder of the team.

If drivers choose team members, they must consider which skill sets and personality traits are required for the product being built or sold. If you are not a driver and are assembling a team, match selected ideas with the personality selection and skills matrix to help determine a "best fit."

For example, a software product would require different skills than a music App for an iPhone. If one of the top 10 ideas is a musical App for the iPhone, and no one on your team has musical skills or knowledge, then the music App idea is not a "best fit" for your team.

However, sometimes passion trumps a skill. In one of our class groups, we determined a potentially winning idea was called Garden on Wheelz™. This idea was a mobile, raised gardening bed. No one on the team was particularly skilled in gardening, but a very enthusiastic team picked up the concept. Would a lack of gardening skills prevent success? Probably not. Can you quickly learn about the basics of gardening? Yes.

There is no real magic to this process and these concepts apply to a group setting and to any entrepreneur starting a business. We know that a healthy mix of all four personalities and a variety of skills will result in a successful business team. Seldom does any one person fit all of the personalities or skills necessary for success. But by using our selection criteria, you can make choices more objectively. Think of it as a trial-and-error approach — something you'll get very good at if you're going to be successful in starting your own business.

Address Ownership of Your New Venture

Once you've formed your team, it is imperative that members have a major discussion at this juncture about ownership. Talk about what ownership means to participants. Not every team member may be an owner. It depends on the circumstances and what the team decides as a group. There are thousands of ways to come together as a team. For example, the idea generator may declare he or she is a founder with a greater piece of the pie. There may be some team members who earn ownership by performance outcomes. Definitely do not give up ownership until you know your partner, or at a minimum, create an easy way out. Dissolving a partnership is much harder than getting rid of an employee or intern.

The team ultimately needs an agreement, in writing, that addresses the following:

- Determine how equity (ownership) shares are distributed.
- Distinguish between partners with ownership, versus employees and/or sub-contractors, as well as what the appropriate circumstances are for the differentiation.
- Determine how much equity owners will attempt to retain. A start-up's founder will make most of his/her money in the long term by the sale of equity (meaning shares or stock).
- Determine the future potential of new owners coming in with investment capital. Stock option plans must be considered.
- Determine how much equity should be reserved for an employee pool. You might want to be able to incentivize and reward good performance as well as have shares available to help recruit top talent.

Don't get bogged down in a lengthy legal discussion of ownership. Team members simply need to derive ownership parameters that they agree are fair, write the agreements down on a piece of paper, and all sign it. We have used a simple partnership template in the past, but we prefer teams construct their own agreements, in their own words. You can find a more formal Partnership Agreement in Appendix C to get some idea of subject matter you need to address in a partnership, but please consult an attorney before using it.

Your choice of entity for your business needs to be addressed at some point. If you begin by forming a simple partnership, you can always change it. In the near future, you may need to address the possibility of forming something more robust with greater liability protection. There are many entity choices (e.g., corporation, limited liability company, partnership) each with their own cost, rules, liability, and tax consequences. When you reach the stage of forming an entity, it's important to obtain approval of the entity by your accountant and lawyer to ensure the entity is the best for your type of business.

Plan on Things Going Wrong

As with any group process, anticipate that things will go wrong, and set some definitive ground rules. In fact, part of this process inherently includes things going wrong. It happens in the classroom in the same way it happens in the real world. Somebody quits a team, someone gets fired for not showing up or doing his or her work, or someone switches teams to work for a competitor. It's an inevitable part of the experience. That is why ground rules and mechanisms for fair termination of a team member are so important. One example of a rule is: If a majority of the team feels a member is not pulling his or her weight, they have the authority to terminate the team member and revert the shares back to the company. And, if a team member quits, she or he forfeits all equity.

The Importance of a Positive Attitude

If there is a single trait all entrepreneurs have in common, it's a positive attitude. We have never met a successful entrepreneur that isn't naturally optimistic. There is no such thing as a negatively minded entrepreneur — negative thinking leads to failure or giving up. Positive thinking is what pushes an entrepreneur through seemingly impossible situations. Entrepreneurs don't just believe they will win, they *know* it.

As you select and build your team, be on the lookout for people who exude "energy," believe in themselves, and remain positive about the future.

We have all heard about the power of positive thinking. From our experience, you need a heavy dose of a positive attitude to succeed in a start-up. When you held a "regular job," you had a job description and a reasonable amount of time to accomplish the focused deliverables related to your job. By contrast, when you work in a start-up company, nothing is "fixed" or "normal." Every day is different. You get up in the morning with your to-do list, and as soon as you begin working, something might rear its ugly head to alter your schedule. You had hoped to accomplish one thing, and instead, you must accomplish three other things first. Confusion, disappointment, and a sense of hopelessness occur — almost as a standard operating procedure for start-up founders.

Yet, to succeed you must stay positive. The driver of the team, in particular, must exude a constant "can do" spirit regardless of how difficult the tasks may seem. We find it beneficial to keep certain sayings on the tip of our tongues, and we repeat them often. Here are some examples:

1. Sure we are afraid, but let's do it anyway.
2. No one wants to get this done more than we do.
3. No problem is too big for us to fix. We can surely find a work around.
4. There is nothing we can't do.
5. This isn't a problem; it's an opportunity to find a solution.
6. People who tell us "No" challenge us even more to get to "Yes."

NOTES

4
Recruit Mentors

In a start-up, it quickly becomes clear to the entrepreneur that he or she needs help, especially when there are little to no funds to pay for outside assistance. You might consider adding experienced partners, or better yet, solicit free help from mentors or advisors. This step guides you through this tangle of decisions and minimizes the chances of getting involved with the wrong people.

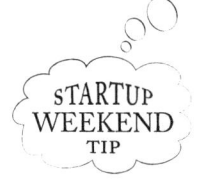

> **STARTUP WEEKEND TIP**
>
> MENTORS ARE KEY PARTICIPANTS AT STARTUP WEEKENDS. TAKE ADVANTAGE OF THEIR AVAILABILITY!

Choosing Mr. (or Mrs.) Right

Selected mentors can be helpful, but be very careful. There are self-touting, egotistical mentors that do not have the right combination of experience or skills to actually be of help, and we have seen some mentors offer help that have no business advising in your industry. The wrong choice of mentors can turn into a huge headache and loss of valuable time. Think of adding mentors to your team in the same way you would hire someone. Carefully choose a mentor in a similar manner that you would create a work team. Make sure each mentor brings a skill set that you do not have yourself, in order to strengthen the team.

WE DEFINITELY NEED SOME ADVICE ON THIS IDEA!
MY PROFESSOR ALWAYS HAS AN OPINION ABOUT EVERYTHING, MAYBE SHE COULD HELP!
MY FRIEND IS AN ENGINEER-TURNED ENTREPRENEUR, WOULD THAT HELP?
WE ALREADY HAVE A CUSTOMER. SHOULD WE INVITE HIM TO HELP?

As you progress in your launch, you may find that different mentors are useful at different times. Or, you may find you have a personality conflict with a mentor. It is okay to change mentors, bring new ones on, and let others fade away.

At the Scheinfeld Center, we bring in mentors of all types. We have a finance expert, a product development expert, a patent attorney, a scientist, a general business and entrepreneur consultant, a marketing expert, and so on. Students gravitate toward different mentors at different times in the process, and some students continue to work with their mentors long after the program is over.

When looking for assistance, ask yourself what type of help you most desperately need. Almost every entrepreneur requires help with financial advising. Other areas may include: product development, manufacturing, sales, distribution, investments, and legal advising, on issues such as intellectual property, contracts, and personnel hiring agreements.

Once you know your needs, decide how many advisors you want to bring in at this stage. Early on, it is advisable to have at least two mentors — one with financial expertise and one with product development expertise.

Note to group leaders: If you are leading a program for students, bring in a variety of mentors and personalities, and make sure they have the appropriate entrepreneurial and start-up experience, as opposed to executive experience.

Here are some questions to ask a mentor:
- Have you been an entrepreneur, as opposed to a corporate executive?
- What kind of business did you run? What are your successes?
- What is your area of expertise?
- Are you a potential investor? Sometimes a potential partner may be less of a match in skills but can bring valuable funds to the start-up company. At some point, a mentor with potential

investment power is worth considering — but with care.
- Do you expect an ownership interest?

This last one is a sticky area. Avoid mentors who engage in high-pressure tactics to influence you to give up equity or who bill for their services. Ideal mentors are there to help you because they are "paying it forward." They experienced success with the help of mentors in their field, and they genuinely want to give back.

However, depending upon the kind of product you are developing, some circumstances warrant a mentor being paid in equity or with a stipend. In general, if you receive funding or some kind of investment to further develop a product, then you may want to consider paying your key advisors with equity and/or money. Whether or not money is involved, consider setting parameters for your relationship with your mentor, such as how often you'll meet (weekly, monthly, etc.) Setting a regular schedule and sticking with it is key to your progress. As you assemble your team members and/or mentors, make sure all team players sign contracts and non-disclosure agreements, which keep you in control. Appendix D contains a sample Non-Disclosure Agreement, but check with your attorney before using it.

NOTES

FlashPals™

Doug Stienstra, Founder

This concept is an example of a "feel good" product, as opposed to solving any pain. It feels good to buy it because it is cute and cuddly, and the company is socially responsible. Mentors played a key role in its development.

The Founder

Doug Stienstra started FlashPals™ when he was 21 years old while studying abroad in southern Brazil. Upon his return, he began taking classes at Iowa State University (ISU). As an "Undecided" major, his diverse interests led him to explore various disciplines and new places. He eventually graduated from the ISU with honors in International Studies and a minor in Business.

Mission Statement > Our mission is to protect what matters most in the world, whether it's data on animals, or deleting ignorance, or just working together to understand each other better.

Company Growth > FlashPals was not even supposed to be a business. My girlfriend at the time wanted a "cute" flash drive for her birthday, and I couldn't find one. So I made my own cuddly flash drive, and she loved it. Amazingly, there was an immediate market for my stuffed animal flash drives. Through the ISU startup incubator, I was able to talk to other entrepreneurs and seek help from mentors. There were a lot of pieces to solve, such as manufacturing, logistics, and ecommerce development, and it all seemed so daunting.

Business Model > Simply put, FlashPals are unique USB flash drives with stuffed animal designs, but in reality, they are much more than that. Each has a keychain to strap onto your backpack, and a heart that lights up when plugged in. More importantly, FlashPals are mascots for bio-diversity. We partner with wildlife organizations to share fascinating "DataBites" about the animals with our audience, while also supporting each organization's efforts

5
Study the Industry

The business world is reasonably well organized into recognizable industries, all possessing special characteristics. You need to become somewhat of an expert in your industry category. In this step, we will help you discover the particulars about the industry in which your product idea best fits, and we will guide you through the key elements of industry analysis and how you can use the research to enhance your product launch.

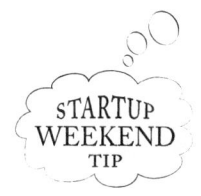

> **STARTUP WEEKEND TIP**
>
> YOU CAN BE PRETTY CONVINCING WITH COMMAND OF JUST A FEW KEY STATISTICS ABOUT YOUR INDUSTRY, AS WELL AS SOME INFORMATION THAT DEMONSTRATES A GAP IN THE MARKET. TO PREPARE YOUR INITIAL PITCH, FIND ONE OR TWO KEY STATS TO HELP SET UP THE PROBLEM YOU ARE GOING TO SOLVE AT THE OUTSET.

Find Key Statistics about Your Industry

A few of the key points in learning about your industry include: category, size, and statistics.

Research: To determine your industry category, we recommend spending a minimum of 4 to 5 hours conducting research on your industry. You want to have a working knowledge of key statistics that define your industry, and you need to know the major players that drive the industry.

The North American Industry Classification System (NAICS) is the standard used by federal statistical agencies in classifying business establishments for the purpose of collecting, analyzing, and publishing statistical data related to the U.S. business economy. You can find your NAICS classification on the census.gov website.

Let's take our Garden on Wheelz™ example. As we mentioned earlier, this is a raised mobile compact gardening bed for people confined to a wheelchair or for older people who want to continue the love of gardening but can no longer stand back up after being on the ground. What is the NAICS classification of the Garden on Wheelz™?

If the company is selling retail from a storefront, it would be categorized as Retail Trade (Sector 44-45), and then subcategorized as Lawn & Garden Equipment & Supply Stores (Sector 4442). Knowing these classifications can help kick-start your research.

Once you know the official name and classification of your industry, you can do a quick Google search on the "Lawn and Garden Industry," and several research reports will pop up, including information that will help you determine the size of your industry. You quickly learn that this industry is a $10 billion retail market in the U.S. alone. While this information does not yet allow you to determine the potential revenue available to your business, it is a good starting point.

This process took just about 3 minutes. If you spend a few hours researching, you can discover the key statistics about your industry that you'll need to help sell your product during a pitch to investors.

Research and gathering vital statistics on the top retailers involves reviewing annual reports of large companies within your field to obtain industry statistics and other useful information. For example, a quick Google search shows that Armstrong Garden Centers is the top retailer in America in this industry, grossing $120 million in annual sales.

Why Industry Information Is Important

This industry information is important because you need to prove to investors and your customers that you possess a command of your market. It's what will make you a great sales agent of your product. You should know the space you are attempting to occupy (in other words, who is sharing the space in your industry), and how large the industry is, in terms of sales.

The latter will help you estimate the market share (percentage of this market in dollars) you can reasonably expect to tap into, based on your particular target or goal. Large corporations in the United States have many divisions and often address multiple product lines. Almost all large corporations are publicly traded, and therefore, much of their detailed financial information is available online. You can find any publicly traded company's financials on the major finance search engines (Yahoo Finance, for example) or on its own website, usually under the investor section. This treasure trove of market information is essential as you plan your entrepreneurial strategy.

Your product idea will undoubtedly fit into one or more of the corporate giants' categories. Finding where your product might fit into a larger company is key to your exit strategy (discussed in more detail in the final step). This same corporate giant might be the one to buy your unique idea, once you have proven the success of your company through strong sales.

As you research, jot down major characteristics of your industry. When considering size of the industry, don't assume you have to be in a large industry to succeed — quite the contrary. It's often preferable to be "a big fish in a small pond" to safeguard your survival.

WE ARE "ECO-CAPITALISTS," IS THERE AN ESTABLISHED INDUSTRY FOR THAT?
WOULD OTHERS FEEL HURT IF WE INVENTED OUR OWN INDUSTRY?

LET'S BE CONSERVATIVE AND PICK AN EXISTING INDUSTRY
BUT ENTREPRENEURS ARE SUPPOSED TO BE AUDACIOUS. LET'S COME UP WITH OUR OWN BOLD AND INVENTIVE NEW IDEAS!

Also take note of where your industry is primarily located geographically. Most industries are located where labor is the least expensive, since more than 70% of a company's budget usually goes to labor costs. In other cases, companies start in (or move to) areas known for specific skills. For example, the high-tech industry exists mostly in the Bay Area/San Jose/Silicon Valley. The automobile industry was mostly located near Detroit until labor unions increased labor prices to a level that these companies moved to "right to work" states, primarily in the South.

Possible Delimiters

Is Your Industry Highly Regulated?

It may seem insignificant when you're "just toying" with product industries, but it's important to know how your industry is regulated. As we mentioned, the food industry is highly regulated, and it can be very tough for a start-up to jump through all the bureaucratic hoops. We recommend shying away from making your first product ingestible. The barriers are too overbearing and make it very difficult to launch rapidly. Choose something outside a heavily regulated industry to test your entrepreneurial muscle before tackling bigger ideas such as food or vitamin products.

Does Your Product Require Expensive Programming?

Technology driven products can also be tricky because they invariably need high-tech teams to develop or engineer the hardware/software, and programmers are not only hard to find, but also command high compensation for their work. High tech can quickly become "high wreck" if it's not done carefully, with focus and the right amount of capital. On the other hand, first mover high-tech products are easier to differentiate from other products, and there is a high motivation to concentrate in this area. For example, software-based businesses can be rapidly scaled and designed to be subscription based (Software-as-a-Service or SaaS) and can garner higher relative acquisition prices. If you are a programmer, you can take advantage of your own skill set and take advantage of the ability to drive a leading-edge technology start-up.

Does Your Product Use Unique or Expensive Materials?

If your product is resource driven, look into the pricing and availability of the resources necessary to manufacture your product. Most products begin with "raw materials," and these may be limited. So resource-driven products could result from scarce raw materials or limited manufacturing ability. Often large competitors own their supply chain. For instance, a coffee retailer, like Starbucks, will have a wholly owned subsidiary in Columbia that supplies much of the coffee beans needed for the barista to serve the best coffee. Ask yourself: Do any of your industry competitors have unique access to necessary resources?

With resource-driven products, be aware that large retailers will not deal with small companies, even if the companies have a unique product in high demand, unless they have proven they can deliver high volumes of the product and keep retail shelves supplied with the needed product.

Does Your Product Require Unique Skills?

As a final assessment in studying your industry (for now), ask yourself if your product requires people with unique skills. This can be a major weakness for a start-up. You as the owner/operator may have unique skills, but to grow quickly, you need access to inexpensive, minimum wage individuals who often have no skills at all, but can be quickly trained to do jobs that vary widely and adjust to immediate demands.

NOTES

6

Target Your Market

The more narrow and focused your target market becomes, the more you will be able to understand it. The better you understand your market, the more likely you can design your product idea to be in high demand. In this step, we present our quick ways to identifying and defining your target market.

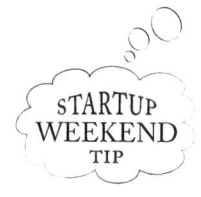

> **STARTUP WEEKEND TIP**
>
> YOU MAY THINK YOU'RE CERTAIN ABOUT WHO YOUR CUSTOMER IS WHEN YOU FIRST PITCH YOUR IDEA ON FRIDAY NIGHT, BUT EXPECT YOUR CUSTOMER AND CONCEPT TO DRAMATICALLY CHANGE BY SUNDAY.

How to Define Your Target Customer

Customers come in all colors, shapes and sizes, so segmenting your target can be challenging. What is the best group to sell your product to? Who is the most likely to open his or her wallet and plunk money down for your product? How many people will pay for it? Will they buy it again and again?

These are questions you really do not know the answer to until you start actually talking with customers. Steve Blank does a great job explaining target market, segmentation, and customer validation concepts on his now ubiquitous and free Udacity lectures on ***How to Build a Start-Up,*** using Alexander Osterwalder's Business Model Canvas tool. We highly recommend his videos, and in this book we give you specific tools to use alongside his lectures to discover your market and customers.

As we saw in the last step, you can gain a lot of information through online searches. But the key to learning about the demographics and psychographics of your potential market will ultimately involve actually talking to potential customers, early and often throughout your development process. However, you need to gather some preliminary data, so for now, look online, and use your personal knowledge to collect demographic and psychographic data.

Demographic data includes: marriage status, annual household income, location, sex, age and family statistics (such as raising children).

To obtain psychographic data ask questions like: What does a typical day in the life of your customers involve? Are they spending more time at work, or at home? Where would they *rather* be? What do they do for fun? Who are the people in their lives that matter most? What kind of cars do they drive? What TV shows do they watch? What clothes do they wear?

How do your customers consume information? How much time do they spend online? What social networks or applications do they use — Facebook? Google? Amazon? Etsy? Do they read newspapers, books or magazines? Which sources do they deem expert, or trust most?

Talk to Your Customers

Once you construct an idea you plan to run with, the next step involves talking to people about your idea. Do people see a need for what you are offering? How do they react when you tell them about your idea? Are they excited? Do they say, "I so needed that yesterday!" Or, do they shrug their shoulders in confusion or indifference? Do they suggest a new and different approach? Would they pay for something similar to what you envision? Who are these people that say they would buy it? Pay attention to them!

We had a student who was developing a bra-fitting service. She made a great case about how nearly 80% of women wear ill-fitted bras, which can cause all sorts of physical problems and potentially serious medical issues. Very early in the conceptual phase, she envisioned making bra-fitting hip, cool and fun and had a great marketing idea to target young women in their 20s. One marketing idea included throwing sorority bra-fitting parties. She wanted to uplift the bra-fitting industry (pun intended) from old and stodgy to young and hip. But when she stood outside a department store and surveyed more than 30 women as they walked in, she discovered women in their 20s could care less about bra-fitting, but women in their 40s and older were very interested. The older set was more concerned about proper bra fittings, as their backs and shoulders hurt, and they experienced posture problems. And so began her customer discovery. When she returned to the classroom, the definition of her target market had completely changed. It went from young, college-aged women in their 20s who have no knowledge of proper bra-fitting to women aged 40 to 65 who were starting to feel the effects of the long-term wear of ill-fitted bras.

Ask More Questions about Your Customers

After you identify your targeted group of customers, consider what makes this group actually *want* to buy your product or service. For example, ask these questions:

1. How much disposable income do typical members of this group have? Disposable income encourages customers to try your product even though their needs may initially be low.
2. What emotions play into their purchase of your product? Buying is often all about emotions — things like: How to I feel about this company? Do I like the image it projects? Does the product make me feel good about buying it? What is the packaging like? Is the company environmentally friendly?

WE ARE LUCKY TO HAVE A VERY FOCUSED AND NARROW TARGET MARKET!
BUT, I HAVE TO SELL OUR PRODUCT, AND THE TARGET MARKET ONLY HAS 376 POTENTIAL BUYERS. THAT'S TERRIBLE!

3. Do the target customers differentiate between brands? This can often be a stumbling point for a start-up product. If your target customers appreciate *value* over brand, they are more likely to give your product a chance. If they are stuck on brand names and tend to be loyal to a particular brand, you could be in trouble.
4. Who is the purchaser in this group? Who has the final say in spending? These questions are often overlooked. For instance, a Home Depot product manager should not assume that a purchase by a man in the store is that man's decision. Research shows that the decision maker behind most household purchases is likely his wife.
5. What values does your typical purchaser have, and how do those values relate to your product? A person's value set is critical in attracting him or her as a new customer. Everything about your product must focus on the customer's value set, and this includes: color, quality, price, guaranteed satisfaction, unique features, and many more things.

Also consider accessibility options for your target customers. If they are internet enabled, you can launch your product by setting up accounts through eBay or Etsy. If you enable customers to purchase online, you often are miles ahead of any other sales channel, because more than half of all products are bought online. If you can ship your product easily, online sales may be the way to go. However, make sure your target customers typically have PayPal or Google Checkout accounts for making online purchases. Ease of paying for your product is essential. PayPal, Amazon, and other online-based paying services are not free, but they are very convenient and very safe.

Consider Geography and Seasonality

Other considerations include whether or not your product is geographically focused and if this is a single-purchase market.

A geographically focused product may be one that works exclusively in a hot climate versus a cold climate. This may also mean that your product is seasonal. Be aware that seasonality can be a big challenge for a start-up company, since it affects cash flow. Consistent cash flow is essential for survival, and running out of cash is a huge mistake that will force your doors to close.

Is This a Single Purchase Product?

Likewise, if your product falls into a single-purchase market, expect difficulty. Repeat customers are key to a successful business. Hopefully, your proposed product has follow-up sales potential, whether it is a repeat purchase item, a subscription, or a way to add upgrades or new features. Many students with an App idea or software concept consider the "freemium" business model, where you tease the customer with a basic version of your product for free, but improved features or upgrades cost money. Or, software can be sold using a subscription based model to attract recurring revenue. Discounts for longer duration commitments can be offered too.

All of the above information, especially demographic and psychographic data, should provide a pretty good handle on the size of your target-customer population. At this stage, all you need is a rough "sizing up" of the customers you want to buy your product.

These steps enable you to zero-in on your particular demographic. Student product developers often mistakenly say: "Everyone is my target customer," but they will quickly discover that no one is their customer with this approach. Your best bet is to begin as a "niche" player with a specific solution to a specific problem experienced by a specific audience of customers.

NOTES

(Left to right) Founders Alexis Ohanian and Steve Huffman

Alexis and Steve are typical of students at SBCC designing social-based Apps and websites with an eye toward eventual philanthropy. Students with programming skills develop prototypes in a single semester.

The Founders

Alexis Ohanian graduated from UVA in 2005, and then started Reddit, now a top 100 website. As a Reddit board member, Alexis also focuses on social enterprise Breadpig, publishing authors like xkcd and SMBC. Profits are donated to worthy causes. He proudly doodled the logos for all three of his startups and loves his cat, Karma.

Steve founded the social news site Reddit in 2005 with his college roommate, Alexis. Reddit has since grown into the largest social news site and one of the largest communities on the Internet.

Mission Statement > From the beginning, the founders said they wanted to be the front page of the Internet.

Company Growth > To see Reddit connecting with so many people around the world has been phenomenal, and the exponential growth we've experienced from the site's founding onwards has been tremendous.

Business Model > Reddit is a platform where people from around the world can share links, stories, pictures and ideas with anyone at any time. Reddit prides itself on it's credo of "all links are created equal," and thus no person's viewpoint or interest is inherently more important than anyone else's. By choosing to either up-vote or down-vote a submission links are moderated by the community; with the things that many people like rising to the top, and less popular submissions sinking to the bottom.

7

Contact Customers

Product ideas are literally a dime a dozen. The challenge is to determine which product idea has the greatest potential for success in the marketplace. In this step, we explore market testing your product ideas and obtaining customer validation.

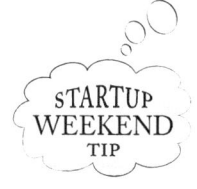

> **STARTUP WEEKEND TIP**
>
> REMEMBER, YOU ARE WORKING FOR YOUR CUSTOMERS, NOT YOURSELF. IF YOUR IDEA IS NOT SOMETHING YOU CAN PROVE A LOT OF PEOPLE WILL PAY FOR, YOU ARE WASTING YOUR TIME.

If you're a fan of Steve Blank and the lean start-up movement, you know by now that "customer validation" is crucial to both the start-up process and taking your next steps. Now that we have screened potential ideas, it's time to put them to the start-up litmus test: Will a lot of people buy this product or service?

Let's step back for a moment and take stock of where we are in the start-up process. At this point, we have some idea of the direction we want to go in, with an idea or two. Before we spend a dime, we want to achieve litmus test number one, and obtain the public's opinion on the idea. However, we need to keep in mind that public feedback is critical throughout the process. At this point, we don't have a prototype. Once you have a crude prototype, you take it out to the public again — that's litmus test number two. As you move along the continuum of the start-up process, check in with your customers, over and over again. The third litmus test involves allowing customers to choose the final product that goes to market.

A note on legal issues: When we begin talking to students about sharing their ideas with the public, they always ask this legal question: If my idea is not protected, don't I risk someone stealing it?" Our answer is: yes. Unfortunately, it is human nature to steal ideas. However, you need to strike a balance between practicality and paranoia, and decide what you can afford to do to protect your idea at such an early phase of validation. Recall that our classroom is a "confidential zone" with NDAs secured. We obtain a lot of objective feedback from each other. When you go out into the public, you can ask people to sign an NDA before taking your survey. Or, for about $100 you can file a preliminary provisional patent. **WARNING — YOU NEED LEGAL ADVICE PRIOR TO FILING WITH THE PATENT OFFICE.** *Once you file a provisional patent, the legal clock starts ticking for you to take the next steps to further your patent, so you need legal advice at this juncture. If you are sitting on some kind of intellectual property, do your own preliminary research at the U.S. Patent and Trademark Office website (USPTO.gov), and then consult with an attorney for the next steps. In the case of Garden on Wheelz™, provisional patents had been filed before he went out to survey the public. Keep in mind, however, that a patent may not provide as much protection as you might assume, because patent infringement cases are expensive. If you cannot afford to enforce infringement, you have no way to protect your intellectual property.*

To prove this point, let's take a look at Garden on Wheelz™ again. Before founder Justin Connell's prototype was ever built, he surveyed a lot of people (including potential customers, namely, older folks) to test the

idea. He asked potential customers a set of questions, including:
1. Do you think a mobile raised gardening bed is a good idea? Why? What are the benefits?
2. What feature would you like to see?
3. What are the possible risks?

The feedback at this early juncture was essential in building a crude prototype that would excite people. During this early phase of customer research, Justin learned that recycling the water from the bottom back into the bed was something people desired. He learned that he might have liability if the gardening bed wasn't stable, so he considered self-locking wheels. Overall, he learned that people loved the idea and found that there was a huge population of older people nationwide that loved gardening but couldn't do it anymore. He also discovered that customers wanted easy and convenient storage for soil and gardening tools.

Gather Informal Feedback from Customers

Research: We recommend spending a minimum of 4 hours outside the classroom talking to customers. Before you hit the streets, you'll need an informal survey and a plan for talking to local target customers to assess interest and gain feedback.

First, choose a realistic sample size of customers that gives you valid results. For example, talk to at least 20 people in your target market each week. Statistically speaking, you need 450 interviews to obtain a valid sample size at a 95% level of accuracy. But at this point, you're looking for high-level feedback, not a scientific study. The scientific studies can come later.

Conduct interviews in a location where your target customer is likely to be. For instance, Baby Boomers ("Boomers") interested in gardening may frequent farmers' markets. This is where Justin conducted his first surveys. In the case of a bra-fitting service, the student surveyed women outside a department store that offered a nice selection of bras.

OKAY, WHERE DO WE FIND POTENTIAL CUSTOMERS?
HOW WOULD YOU FEEL ABOUT RECRUITING PEOPLE ON THE STREET TO LISTEN TO OUR PITCH?

YOU CAN COUNT ME OUT, I'LL BE HERE WORKING ON OUR ACCOUNTING REPORT. THE NUMBERS LOOK TERRIBLE THIS MONTH!
HEY, THIS IS MY GIG. I SUGGEST WE BOOK A BOOTH AT THIS WEEK'S FARMERS' MARKET

As you conduct interviews with strangers, be informal and "chat" about your idea without using a structured survey. If possible, have either a sample of your product or a CAD drawing (even a hand-drawing will do) to show people. Try not to write comments down while interviewing. People love to "chat" but can become nervous when they see you document their words. Plan a free-flow interview, followed by writing down specific comments and overall impressions after the potential customer is gone.

Create a More Formal Survey Based on Informal Feedback

After you've conducted your informal surveys, and as you move into the prototype phase, create more formal surveys for your product. Analyze the information gathered from your informal surveys to extract a pattern of answers. Let this preliminary feedback be your guide in expanding your survey and creating follow-up questions.

Your formal survey can have a list of about 10 to 20 questions, depending on your product. Use multiple-choice answers and "Yes or No" questions. Use a familiar grading system to inquire about features. Most Americans are familiar with the school grading system of A through F. If you use a familiar grading system, you save time and no further explanation is needed. Do not use open-ended questions, which result in long-winded answers that are difficult to interpret. Closed-ended questions, such as multiple choice or "Yes or No," are simple for the customer to respond to and simple for you to record and analyze.

Questions should be drafted with the results you intend to obtain and should be short and to the point. Use questions like: "Would you buy this product if it were available — Yes or No?" or "How much would you consider paying for this product if it were available? A. $10-20; B. $20-30; C: $30-40; D. $40-50?"

Formulate questions about features. To help you do this, make an exhaustive list of descriptive words. To create a comprehensive word list, cast a wide net while searching the Internet for competitive products. Select words that describe your product and what it does. With these descriptive words, you'll ask people which features they like and which are "must have" features vs. "nice to have" features.

Once you have created a more formal survey, take the survey outside and ask customers these questions face-to-face. Pay attention to the feedback you receive when you have the customers' attention, and ask follow-up questions. If they don't like something, ask, "why not?" Ask what they would like better. Ask what feature(s) would make this an exciting product for them. You want to learn from your customer what product you should be making. This is a ***customer-driven*** process. It is a shock to many new entrepreneurs to discover that as early as the invention phase, they need to be listening to real customers and designing for the customer, not themselves.

Once you have completed your surveys, evaluate your product idea based upon the feedback. Did your product garner overall positive customer feedback? You might be onto something potentially successful if initial feedback is overwhelmingly positive. This is an indicator to continue putting in time, effort, and money.

To Proceed or Not to Proceed? That Is the Question!

Based on customer feedback, ask yourself: "Should I continue to spend time and/or money on the development of this product?" If customers' feedback is overwhelmingly positive, then yes, you should proceed. If, on the other hand, you are overwhelmed by how off-track you seem to be based on the feedback, then consider scrapping the concept now before you invest anymore energy, time and money.

If you decide to proceed, then ask: "Does this product require a lot of up-front investment?" If it's $10,000 or less, our vote is a go. Anymore than that, and you will have an uphill battle.

[Positive Feedback? Yes!] [Requires Less Than 10K? Yes!] [Proceed!]

Figure 7-1. To Proceed or Not to Proceed

Most first-time start-up entrepreneurs don't have a lot of money and often don't have a measurable track record. As a result, most investors shy away from investing in first-time businesses. The cornerstone of our rapid start-up philosophy is *crawl, walk, and then run*. Why do we encourage you to start with a small (but scalable) idea? It costs less, it takes less time, you need little upfront cash, and you will attract investors if you have proven sales and a quick return on investment. We want to ensure your first start-up idea is small, realistic, and requires very little upfront investment. If you can make this one a success, your second, and possibly bigger, idea will be more attractive to investors. The goal is to create a proven track record with one small success.

Obviously, the less investment you need, the better. However, there is a delicate balance here. You can't skimp too much on money. Underfunded start-ups frequently fail simply because they run out of money. It might help keep costs down if you do all the legwork in advance, and only bring investors in at the moment you need them. The sooner you can return the investor's money, the better. A typical investor would like to see his/her money back in 1 to 3 years maximum — and at a relatively high rate of return. The higher the multiple of the investor's money you return, the better it is for your start-up reputation. Many investors are constantly in search of proven entrepreneurs who can turn their investments into multiples. If you follow this philosophy, you will be well on your way to proving yourself as a solid investment choice.

As we move into the legal discussion of how to protect your idea, be mindful of how all of your efforts from here on out are to effectively prove to an investor you have a marketable idea.

8
Protect Your Ideas

The world is full of copycat entrepreneurs that will gladly steal your product idea, if you let them. People working in companies can be worse — they are naturally predatory, acting under a veil of being competitive. In this step, we will outline the actions you must take to protect your product idea as securely as possible, given both time and financial limitations.

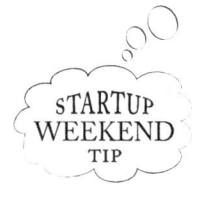

> **STARTUP WEEKEND TIP**
>
> IT IS UNREALISTIC TO THINK YOU WILL BE ABLE TO PROTECT YOUR IDEA FOR YOUR WEEKEND PITCH. ON THE STARTUP WEEKEND WEBSITE THEY SIMPLY SAY YOU CAN'T PREVENT PEOPLE FROM STEALING YOUR IDEA, AND THEY SUGGEST KEEPING KEY PROPRIETARY INFORMATION SECRET AND LEFT OUT OF YOUR PITCH.

We won't get too bogged down in legal considerations. We recognize that there are issues and concerns in this area, and we simply want to highlight these to help raise your awareness about what you may need to watch out for before you start sharing your ideas. Much of the information we share here can be found on USPTO.gov and copyright.gov websites. They are both excellent sources of information. We cannot stress enough the need to seek legal advice from a lawyer with specific knowledge in this area, preferably a patent attorney.

Since we are not practicing attorneys, we cannot give you specific legal advice. We suggest using this step as a guide to help you identify what issues you may need to address with a lawyer. Intellectual Property Law is a vast subject, but let's take a look at the efforts our students have made to help protect their ideas, in hopes that it will help you too. Again, there is only one way to be sure your idea is protected, and that is to work under the advice and guidance of a patent attorney.

Two Simple Practices

There are two very simple practices to begin at the outset, and they are:
1. Write the word "Confidential" on every page of everything you do related to your product development. It may not be solid legal protection, but it gives people notice that what they are looking at is confidential, and it might help you in a future legal battle.
2. Keep an old-fashioned written diary of all meetings, both in person and on the phone, indicating the date, the topic, and the person with whom you spoke. Make sure the other person is aware that you are taking notes of all-important details during the discussion, including who made what commitments. This written "diary," kept in a notebook, is your antidote to a terrible mental disease called "convenient amnesia." When the chips are down, and people say, "I don't remember saying that," you reach for your diary and show them your notes. It's amazing how it will suddenly jar their memory and cure them of amnesia.

Three Main Concerns

There are really three overarching concerns related to idea protection when you are developing a product: trademark/service mark, copyright, and patent. These are three types of intellectual property protection, but they are different and serve different purposes:

Trademarks include any word, name, symbol, or device, or any combination, used, or intended to be used, in commerce to identify and distinguish the goods of one manufacturer or seller from goods manufactured or sold by others. They also indicate the source of the goods. Service marks include any word, name, symbol, device, or any combination, used, or intended to be used, in commerce, to identify and distinguish the services of one provider from services provided by others, and to indicate the source of the services.

Copyrights protect literary, artistic, and musical works. For general information, publications and other copyright related topics, visit http://www.copyright.gov.

Patents protect inventions and improvements to existing inventions.

Let's take a closer look at the three.

Trademark/Service Mark

For any terminology you create, you can add the superscript initials™ and begin claiming it as a trademark. We advise our students to begin using the superscript immediately — on everything. But beware that:
- Others may dispute your claim because you are not fully protected by using ™. You can register your trademark for the best protection (this costs money) and use ®, which indicates a Registered Trademark.
- The date you begin using the ™ on your words and/or phrases is important in establishing ownership.
- If you do nothing, someone can easily "steal" your special product names and tag lines.

Examples of things to trademark are:
- Any special names you create for your company and/or its divisions.
- Any unique names you have created for your product or service.
- Any tag line that is used in conjunction with your product or service.
- Any logos you create.

Copyright

The official definition of a copyright is a form of protection provided by the laws of the United States (title 17, U. S. Code) to the authors of "original works of authorship," including literary, dramatic, musical, artistic, and certain other intellectual works. This protection is available to both published and unpublished works. For detailed information on copyrights, go to www.copyright.gov. Note: Copyright does not protect ideas.

In terms of copyrights, the "practical" action to take is: On any written document or website you create for formal distribution to anyone, just add the word "copyright" with the year, such as 2014. You do not have to register your copyright to be protected, because a copyright is protected the moment it is created. However, to enforce your rights, and for other reasons, you have to register your work.

You should copyright all brochures and flyers describing your product, as well as all papers you write about your product.

The copyright notice should include the date of the first year of use, the owner, and the word "copyright," or the symbol ©.

For example: Add ***Copyright 2002 © John Doe*** to the bottom footer of every page you produce about your product.

Patent

The official definition of a patent is an intellectual property right granted by the Government of the United States of America to an inventor "to exclude others from making, using, offering for sale, or selling the invention throughout the United States or importing the invention into the United States" for a limited time in exchange for public disclosure of the invention when the patent is granted.

There are three types of patents. Utility patents may be granted to anyone who invents or discovers any new and useful process, machine, article of manufacture, or composition of matter, or any new and useful improvement thereof. Design patents may be granted to anyone who invents a new, original, and ornamental design for an article of manufacture. Plant patents may be granted to anyone who invents or discovers and asexually reproduces any distinct and new variety of plant.

Upon request, the U.S. Patent and Trademark Office (USPTO) will send information on utility and design patent applications, including forms for filing applications. To request this information, contact the USPTO Contact Center (UCC), and request to be transferred to the Inventors Assistance Center (IAC).

International Protection: Many countries are part of Patent Cooperation Treaty (PCT) that provides a unified procedure for filing patents internationally. The granting of a patent is the prerogative of the particular country or granting authority for a particular region. Check with your patent attorney on whether you need protection internationally.

Disclosure: Since a key element of claiming protection under a patent is novelty, public disclosure prior to protection can affect your ability to obtain a U.S. or foreign patent. Here is a link to an informative article on disclosure: http://www.grad.wisc.edu/research/ip/publicdisclosure.html. Always check with a patent attorney before making any disclosure.

Some of our students began the process of protecting their ideas by filing a provisional patent, based on the advice of a patent attorney. This permits the student to use the phrase: "Patent Pending." There can be a problem if you file too early (without enough funding to complete the application) because a 12-month clock starts ticking, and if you don't complete the non-provisional application, you will lose pendency status and all protection.

The official definition of a provisional application is a patent application, which establishes an official United States patent application filing date

WE REALLY NEED TO APPLY FOR A PATENT TO PROTECT OUR PRODUCT!
Patent Pending

I CAN PREPARE ALL THE DETAILS TO DEFINE THE UNIQUENESS OF OUR PRODUCT, INCLUDING PICTURES
Patent Pending
PERFECT, WHEN CAN YOU HAVE THAT DONE?

for the invention and permits the term *"Patent Pending"* to be applied in connection with the invention. A foreign application may claim priority to a provisional application.

A provisional application automatically becomes abandoned when its pendency expires ***12 months after*** the provisional application filing date, by operation of law. Applicants must file a non-provisional application claiming benefit of the earlier provisional application filing date in the USPTO *before* the provisional application pendency period expires in order to preserve any benefit from the provisional-application filing.

You can find information on provisional applications at: http://www.uspto.gov/web/offices/pac/provapp.htm.

Provisional patents have worked well for some of our students who needed to protect their designs and processes and later attained funding to complete the process in a timely manner. (We were fortunate enough to have a registered USPTO attorney helping us!)

The filing fee for a provisional patent can be as low as $65 and as high as $260. A detailed written description of your product is required, and, most likely, a set of drawings of your product. Again, it is critical to check with a patent attorney on what you need to include. The provisional application must be properly and broadly set up in anticipation for your future non-provisional application.

To apply for a provisional patent, you can go to the U.S. Patent office website, and submit your credit card payment — but again, it is best to seek the advice of an attorney to know what to include in your application.

By applying for a provisional patent, you're protected within the parameters of the system with the ability to use "Patent Pending" status, (which tends to impress investors). You also establish public awareness of your product idea. But don't forget, this can be a double-edged sword — and disastrous — if you fail to follow up with the more expensive non-provisional application within 12 months.

Even if you file for a provisional patent, and follow up with the non-provisional application, no amount of protection is worth anything without funding to enforce it. In other words, your intellectual property rights might technically be protected, but if someone infringes, and you have no funding to hire lawyers and sue for infringement, you're out of luck. Therefore, many small companies sometimes prefer to focus their attention in the beginning on sales and increasing market share, as opposed to committing time and expense towards patent filing. But the value of your intellectual property is a tangible asset that can be leveraged for investment funding, and most investors will want to see that you have taken steps to protect this property.

Non-Disclosure Agreements

As previously mentioned, we create a "confidential zone" in the classroom using a Non-Disclosure Agreement (NDA) attached as Appendix D. Again, we have the good fortune of an attorney working pro bono to help students in the classroom. We highly recommend you reach out to your local patent attorneys and ask them to be a pro bono mentor in your program by explaining your need. Most people become enthusiastic to participate because of the sheer joy and excitement of the program — plus it could lead to future paid business.

An NDA is an agreement signed by the person you plan to tell about your product idea. Legal points a typical NDA should address are:
- Name of the person signing the NDA,
- date of the NDA signing, and
- language to the effect that the person signing it will not disclose anything about your product idea to anyone, for a limited period of time.

To prepare an NDA, it is always best to hire an attorney to draft an NDA for your specific purposes. Having said that, there are numerous online sources for NDA templates, including Legal Zoom, Nolo Press, and Rocket Lawyer.

Once you obtain an NDA, make sure you and the person(s) to whom you plan to present your idea sign the NDA *before* any discussion, especially regarding the details of your idea, takes place. Though it may be tempting, never discuss your idea casually at a party, or with friends, without an NDA. Doing so could be considered a public disclosure and could ruin a future patent application. In addition, your friends may "unknowingly" tell others less trustworthy, and as we have already indicated, people are ruthless in "stealing," as it is human nature.

If you intend to seek funds from investors, many are offended when asked to sign an NDA. In these circumstances, use your best judgment. You likely don't want to risk losing a potential qualified investor over this issue.

9
Analyze the Competition

Find and be able to name the companies that occupy the same or similar space in the industry. There is no product idea with "no competitors." Even if you really are a first-mover, there will be others in the industry with the ability to run with your idea faster, better, and cheaper. In this step, we show you how to do a thorough search of the competition.

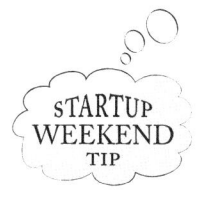

> **STARTUP WEEKEND TIP**
>
> THE WORST PRACTICE IS TO SAY YOU HAVE NO COMPETITORS. DON'T EVER SAY THAT. THERE ARE ALWAYS COMPANIES IN YOUR "SPACE," AND YOU NEED TO KNOW WHO THEY ARE.

Admit You Have Competitors

The first step involves admitting you have competitors. The biggest mistake start-ups make is maintaining a mindset that there are no competitors. Perhaps this is "technically" true, especially if you are a first-mover or if you are improving upon an existing idea that truly differentiates it from the old idea. However, investors want to know that you have researched your space, and simply telling them you have no competitors won't cut it. You need to point out the sellers in your industry with "similar" products or concepts.

I AM SO BUMMED! I JUST SAW OTHER PRODUCTS WITH THE SAME FEATURES AND IN THE SAME PRICE RANGE!

BUT, OUR PRODUCT WILL BE FASTER, LIGHTER, AND MORE DURABLE. DOESN'T THAT MAKE A BIG DIFFERENCE?
WELL, WE COULD BUILD OUR PITCH AROUND THAT!

View Your Product Objectively

You can't improve your product until you recognize what's wrong with your product in the first place. Admitting your product isn't the most original idea ever conceived humbles you and enables you to see what other companies have done so far. Your research will help show you what others have done wrong and point out what others have missed. Then, you can truly evaluate your product to see whether or not it's innovative enough to be competitive. Studying your competition also begins to provide a benchmark of pricing and sales volume.

Revisit Your Industry Analysis

Remember when we asked you to name the top company in your industry? Go back to that company's website and study it. Look at how many lines of product it offers. Evaluate which product line your product would fit. Decide what product the company produces is most similar to yours. Compare their products' features to yours, and begin a comparison grid (Table 2). You will use this grid for other company and product comparisons as you find more competitors. As you uncover features other products have but yours doesn't, add them to the features list.

If we use Garden on Wheelz™ as an example in the chart below, you can see that competitors exist, but none offer all the features of Justin's product. You can easily see the variants just by looking at the pictures of each competitor's design.

Table 2. Evaluation of Competitor Features

Feature ▶ Product ▼	Recycles Water	Adjustable Height	Rot Resistant	Durable Rubber?	Portable?	Self-locking Wheels
Garden on Wheelz™	Yes	Yes	Yes	Yes	Yes	Yes
Accessible Gardens™	Yes	No	Yes	No	Yes	No
VegTrug™	No	No	No	No	Yes	No

Analyze the Competition

Figure 9-1. Garden on Wheelz™

As you continue your competitor research, conduct specific online searches to uncover your competitors. Do variable keyword searches to discover all competitors.

Don't just stop with a couple keyword searches or website reviews. Be diligent and thorough. Competition comes in many forms and sizes. It's best to derive keyword searches to make your search relevant. Here is our grid for sorting out our keyword searches for Garden on Wheelz™ and keeping a record of potential competitors to research even further (Table 3).

Table 3. Competitor Key Word Search

Key Words	Potential Competitor List
Raised Garden Bed	Rustic Elevated Garden Bed (Garden.com)
Mobile Garden	Elevated Garden Bed (Home Depot); Mobile Garden Table (Bed, Bath & Beyond)
Wheelchair Garden	Accessible Edible Garden — Lazy Susan (article in LATimes — designer Laramee Haynes); TerraForm by LaValise
Adjustable Garden Bed	Nomad Raised Garden Bed with Adjustable Legs (Wagle.com)

We suggest you visit local stores (or drive to the nearest big city) to see if they sell anything locally that you can inspect. For Justin, we recommended he visit local nurseries and Home Depot, as well as look through gardening catalogs. When you find a product that serves a similar purpose, take pictures and make a note of price, construction design, materials, features, and labeling.

Figure 9-2. VegTrug™

Figure 9-3. Accessible Gardens

Figure 9-4. Nomad™

Analyze the Competition

Research: We recommend spending a minimum of 4 hours on competitive research. When you have completed your research, you will choose the top three competitors that are most closely aligned with your product and create a detailed comparison grid, listing every possible feature. Eventually you will highlight the top 10 differentiating features you plan to pursue for your product. Hang onto this grid. It will be useful in the next step and may be useful in the end to refine and use as a visual in your pitch presentation.

NOTES

Analyze the Competition

10
Differentiate

*Seth Godin's **Purple Cow: Transform Your Business By Being Remarkable** suggests that in order to stand out in an oversaturated marketplace, you need a remarkable product that people talk about. Do you and/or your product stand out? This step helps you find your product's distinctive advantage.*

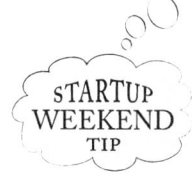

> **STARTUP WEEKEND TIP**
>
> KNOW YOUR "UNIQUE SELLING PROPOSITION"(USP) PRIOR TO PITCHING.

After spending some time identifying your competitors, you should have some sense of how you plan to make your product different so that it stands out from the competition.

Once you identify your top three competitors and note each product feature in the comparison grid, look at the following potential differentiating factors of your competitors.

DO YOU HAVE ANY IDEAS HOW WE CAN MAKE OUR PRODUCT REALLY DIFFERENT?
U.S.P.

OUR PRODUCT FEELS GOOD' TO THE CUSTOMER BECAUSE IT IS MADE FROM ECO-FRIENDLY MATERIALS. SO, COULD WE BUILD ON THAT?
U.S.P.
DEFINITELY. OUR PRODUCT BOTH SOLVES A CUSTOMER'S PROBLEM, BUT WE ALSO MAKE THE CUSTOMER FEEL GOOD ABOUT BUYING IT. YOU'RE A GENIUS!

Unique Operating Characteristics

First, study a business' operating characteristics. One example of a company that stands out with its unique business characteristics is Patagonia. Its founder, Yvon Chouinard, explained to the Scheinfeld Center that Patagonia takes its impact on the environment so seriously and purposely keeps growth slow and low. Being a responsible company is more important than the bottom line, and yet the company is still extremely successful. Why? Its philosophy, coupled with authentic behavior aligned with that philosophy, makes up its USP. This is how Patagonia is remarkable.

Other important characteristics to notice include whether or not the companies are:
- public or private,
- big or small,
- for profit or nonprofit, and
- uniquely driven by a philosophy.

Unique Marketing Platforms

After you acquire this basic information, analyze the companies' marketing strategies, which make some companies unique. One example is Web Marketing Therapy, a full-service marketing firm. Its founder, Lorrie Thomas, created a company with a very strong brand, even though it only has a virtual presence. Her model eradicates the perception that you need brick and mortar to be legitimate. She has a unique set of core values that evolved from listening to her customers. Her customers expressed overwhelming relief to have found someone to fix their online marketing issues, and they told her it felt like therapy! She embraced this USP to benefit her company, and it single-handedly drives her brand.

Another company with a unique marketing strategy is Tom's Shoes. Its founder, Blake Mycoskie, decided that for every pair of shoes he sold to the public, he would donate one pair of shoes to someone in need in a developing country. It was a brilliant idea, derived from his own personal observations of need while traveling in Argentina. "One for One" is his USP, and it makes both him and his product remarkable.

Unique Distribution or Sales Strategies

In addition to studying operations and marketing strategies, review companies' distribution and sales strategies. Some questions to answer about businesses include whether or not they:
- use classic, traditional advertising (through media outlets),
- are predominantly Internet based,
- mostly rely on social-media,
- possess a unique way of delivering a service or even packaging, and
- employ philosophy driven marketing and advertising.

Also look at whether or not the products are:
- built to order,
- distributed through a warehouse,
- offered in company stores,
- involved in general merchandizing, and/or
- part of a company culture that pervades every aspect of delivery.

One company that has developed a unique culture of selling in the wine industry is Barefoot Wine. The founders, Michael Houlihan and Bonnie Harvey, shared information about their USP — The Barefoot Spirit — with the Scheinfeld Center. They put genuine care and personalized attention into every aspect of the business, including the distribution and sales process. When they ran up against distribution problems, the owners visited distribution centers and talked to the forklift drivers. The personalized Barefoot Spirit is what makes their company remarkable.

Sales strategies of your competitors are essential to study. The founders of Barefoot Wine began a winery from scratch, with no experience. They needed to build awareness of their brand, so they began selling through worthy causes. They sponsored events for fundraisers and other important events (one of their first causes aptly was the Surfrider Foundation), and this became their unique selling tactic: grassroots brand awareness.

Other sales strategies include:
- boots on the ground, guerilla marketing and/or hiring sales professionals,

- third-party representation, and
- brick-and-mortar retail stores.

As you do your research, look at possible barriers to entry for potential competitors, such as:
- patent pending,
- first-mover advantage,
- a unique brand and reputation,
- market share and
- the ability to create more "buzz."

You are better positioned to overcome existing barriers to entry if you have more money from investors, extraordinary people skills, a large customer backing you, or other business advantages.

After you have analyzed your competition through all of the above lenses, consider how you will distinguish your product and your company from the competition. Perhaps you fall short in some areas but excel in others. Decide what characteristics are most important to enable your business to succeed and take stock of where your idea already beats the competition.

For example, do you provide more features or a better quality than already existing products? Do you offer them at a lower price? Does your company employ unique distribution methods or grassroots selling models? Do you excel at comprehensive service or ease of accessibility or terms? Do you offer longer warranties or back your product with guaranteed satisfaction, or your money back? And what are your personal philosophies and experiences — your story — that you bring to your company?

A challenging exercise students enjoy is: "Describe Your Product or Service in Only Six Words." This forces students to use only words that have the most value in explaining what they do or what their product does. Sometimes, their unique selling proposition becomes apparent after this exercise. Groups can help crystallize descriptions by offering ideas and positive feedback, as well as critiquing each other.

(Left to right) Founders Kevin Petrovic, Rujul Zaparde and Shri Ganeshram

These young founders are changing the car rental industry with a simple, but scalable business model. Audacious and fearless, they are taking on major competitors without a second thought.

The Founders

As co-founder and CEO, 18-year old Rujul Zaparde, is in the driver seat as FlightCar takes off in Boston. Inspired by the high cost and hassle of getting to and from the airport, he and co-founder Kevin Petrovic had the unique idea that peer-to-peer car sharing could be used to offer free parking for consumers who are leaving town; and for visitors, it could provide a better and less expensive car rental experience.

At 19 years old, co-founder and COO Kevin Petrovic is the eldest among FlightCar's three co-founders. An entrepreneur since age 9, Kevin dropped out of Princeton University to devote his time to FlightCar, which he sees as revolutionizing the way people get to and from the airport.

As CTO, 18-year old co-founder Shri Ganeshram is responsible for making FlightCar's unique model of peer-to-peer airport car-sharing work online. Shri dropped out of Massachusetts Institute of Technology, after his first year of college to start FlightCar.

Mission Statement > The company's goal is to provide a resource where airline travelers can list their car for use by someone else while they are gone. The mission of the company is to solve the problem of expensive airport parking and airport car rentals, and in the process reduce airport congestion and waste.

Company Growth > The company is laying the ground work and infrastructure for rapid growth in the future.

Business Model > FlightCar is a unique new car-sharing business focused on the airport customer with the goal of an overall improvement in a traveler's experience. Vehicle owners drop off their cars at the FlightCar parking lot, located near major airports, and are then taken to the airport in a black car/limo. While they are away, they have guaranteed free parking and get a free carwash and cleaning. They can also make money based on how long their car is rented. Travelers coming in to that same airport can rent the same vehicle for a significant savings over a traditional rental car company.

11
Build Your Prototype

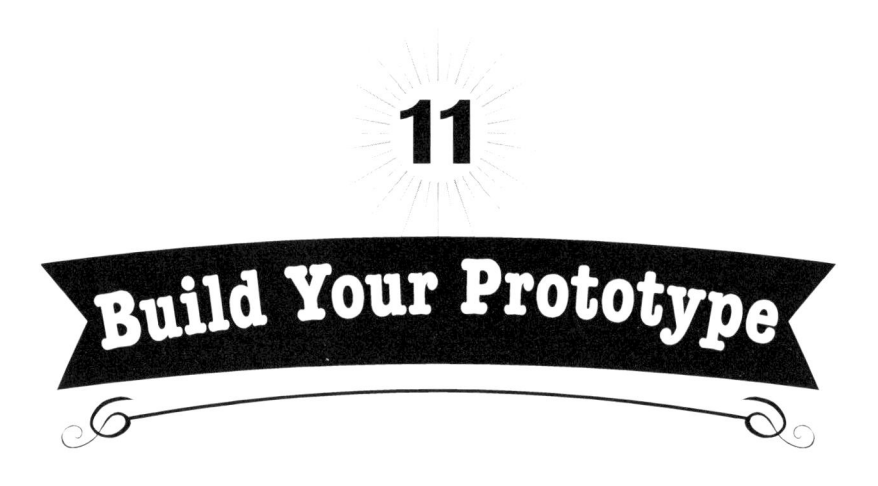

At some point, you must transition from your product idea to the real thing, namely a prototype. In some cases, a prototype may be an actual physical manifestation of your product. In other cases, it may simply be an artist rendition of your idea. The key is to create something that potential customers or investors can see and evaluate. In this step, we will explore various ways to create a prototype of your product idea.

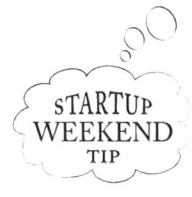

> **STARTUP WEEKEND TIP**
>
> YOU LIKELY WON'T HAVE THE TIME TO BUILD A PROTOTYPE DURING THE WEEKEND UNLESS YOU'RE LUCKY ENOUGH TO HAVE ACCESS TO 3D PRINTING OR HAVE A DEVELOPER TO CREATE A DEMO VERSION OF YOUR APP. IF YOU'RE NOT SO LUCKY, SIMPLY FOCUS ON CREATIVELY SKETCHING IDEAS AND FEATURES.

Essential Aspects to Consider in Creating an Initial Prototype

At this stage, you should not be trying to make something to sell. Your first prototype is far from the final product. This initial prototype will become an "artifact" demonstrating the history of the evolution of the product. Remember, there should be several more rounds of customer validation after you create your first and second prototypes. Consider this a rough mock-up to help you explain what you plan to manufacture. If your idea involves a service, your prototype could be a mock-up of a webpage.

The purpose of making your first prototype is twofold:
1. It helps you determine how realistic your concept is. This initial prototype may demonstrate that it can work, or, on the other hand, that your idea is more complex than you originally imagined. It sets the stage for a possible pivot to another idea, or to your second version.
2. It creates a demonstration for further customer validation. Now you have something to show a customer.

Use Cheap, Accessible Materials

If your idea is viable, you will need this first-phase prototype to help interest both investors and customers in your product. People react to seeing something tangible. If it's possible, it is best to show an early rendition of your product using cheap materials, as opposed to mere drawings. A physical manifestation goes a long way in helping investors and customers understand your concept much better. And, a better understanding encourages more accurate investor and customer feedback.

Ty Blunt, one of our students who invented the NAK™ (a nail accessory kit) spent several sessions pitching his idea to the class. Almost out of sheer frustration of no one really understanding what his concept looked like, he gathered nail-grooming tools from his roommates and girlfriend. Then he used a torch and solder in his bedroom (not recommended) to construct his first prototype. It was an extremely crude version of something that he would refine again and again. However, it was the perfect first prototype! When he shared it with the class, we clearly saw his vision and gave him valuable feedback.

We've had students sew, knit, solder, sketch, paint, glue, nail and use computer-generated drawings. Whatever is at your disposal, use it. But please be *safe*.

Spend Less Than $300

If you are developing a program for students, one way to enable the prototype phase is to invite a benefactor/donor to help. We have an entrepreneur-in-residence who pays for the making of crude, inexpensive prototypes. Each student team has an approximate budget of $300. You can build what you need for less than that. If you have a little funding, here are some things to consider:

First, decide what kind of physical materials you need to build a prototype. If it's wood, for example, find the least expensive wood to use. Cost compare at various stores (both online and brick-and-mortar), and determine the best place to purchase materials.

If you don't have the skills to work with the physical materials in order to build your prototype, identify someone who does. Ask yourself what skills are needed and where you can find people with these skills (such as woodworking, metalsmithing, or printing). You may be able to find skilled people who are willing to donate a bit of their time or participate for extremely low cost. Out-of-work contractors or laborers are good people to ask. Post an ad on Craigslist or TaskRabbit asking for the talent you need.

If your business involves a service rather than a product, mock up an ad or brochure, or build a webpage for it. (If you are working on a product but can't find the resources to build it, you can do the same with print ads or webpages.) Either way, it's helpful to build a quick, preliminary template of your product or service on a website or blog. There are plenty of free web and blog services, including Weebly, Blogger, and Word-Press.

Keep in mind the eventual evolution of quality. Once you create the first sample, don't stop there: Begin to consider your next version. Think about using different and/or better materials, and make notes of your dream prototype. But, while imagining your future version, remember to be patient with yourself and the process. You may or may not get the opportunity to build a perfect prototype, but this crude version has the potential to secure funding to get there!

WE ALL SEEM TO AGREE TO WHAT OUR PRODUCT SHOULD DO AND WHAT IT WILL LOOK LIKE. NOW WHAT?
WE COULD MAKE A SKETCH ON A NAPKIN?

WITH MY CAD PROGRAM I CAN MAKE A VERY REALISTIC LOOKING PROTOTYPE!
I AM PRETTY HANDY WITH TOOLS SO I COULD MAKE A PROTOTYPE IN MY GARAGE!

Feeling Like It's Obsolete Already?

In the next step we discuss how to obtain feedback on your first prototype. Be forewarned that based on feedback, you immediately begin to understand how to refine your prototype in the future. In fact, the minute your first prototype is complete, you may feel as if it is already obsolete. That's okay. Believe us when we say it's progress! Ty was almost embarrassed to share his crude prototype after a while because his vision of the final product was so sleek — and his prototype was very bulky. From our standpoint, his first prototype was so impressive because it told a story about Ty and his determination.

At this stage, simply jot down a list of features you intend to include in the second iteration. You may not have the funds yet to build your ideal version, but now you can show your original prototype with a list of potential features and perhaps a second-generation sketch. Having a crude prototype coupled with a list of potential features is much better than a drawing or nothing at all, and you will likely impress potential investors. You will be able to gauge how interested investors are, and their feedback enables you to narrow down where and how you will obtain funding to develop the product.

Your first prototype makes a huge impact on an audience — whether it be peers, investors or potential customers — and that impact is immeasurable. To investors, in particular, they not only see the product, but they also see your dedication. It could be what tips the scale toward your first investment.

12
Evolve Your Prototype

In an ideal world, your prototype evolves from your initial vision to the vision of your target customers. You do not design the best products — your customers design winning products. In this step, we show you how to get your customers intimately involved in your product evolution.

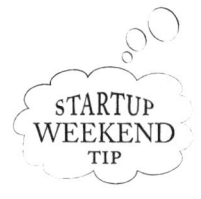

> **STARTUP WEEKEND TIP**
>
> THIS PART OF YOUR WORK INVOLVES "PIVOTING." BASED ON CUSTOMER FEEDBACK, YOUR IDEA CAN COMPLETELY CHANGE FROM YOUR FIRST PITCH ON FRIDAY NIGHT. BY SUNDAY, THE AUDIENCE WILL MARVEL AT HOW YOU EVOLVED.

Take Stock & Consider Scrapping Your Idea, Again

It is time, once again, to decide whether to scrap the idea, or to run with it. Let's take a moment to review what we have learned so far and evaluate where you stand. Now is the time to decide whether you really believe in your product and really want to move forward — with passion.

Answer these questions truthfully:
- Has your concept evolved from your original concept? Why? Was it based on feedback from other people? Who?

- Did you have to scale back your idea from what you originally thought you could accomplish?
- Is there another idea in the group that seems to have momentum and a lot of excitement? Would you rather work with that team and let your idea go for now?
- Does this process involve way more work than you expected?
- How have your perceptions and expectations of the process changed?
- Are you more or less focused?

Figure 12-1. To Proceed or Not to Proceed

What do your answers tell you? If you are more focused and more passionate about your idea now than you were when you started, you are ready to move ahead. If, on the other hand, you are having second thoughts or feeling discouraged by customer feedback, then you might consider scrapping your idea. **Sometimes the most valuable lesson in this evaluative process involves learning what ideas are not worth pursuing, for whatever reason.** There are some very good reasons to scrap an idea that doesn't seem as good as when you started. For instance, realizing your ego got over involved and you became fixated on an idea simply because you thought of it is not a good reason to move forward. Another example involves a strong urge to ignore feedback from potential customers. The market is your best teacher, and if it's telling you to try something else, it's best to listen. Finally, if you're in a group setting and you find yourself more interested in another team's idea, it's best to join forces with those members rather than holding onto an idea you're not as excited about.

If you end up abandoning your idea, don't view it as a waste of time. Rather, think of all the time, effort and money you saved by scrapping a "bad," or unviable idea.

It's best to devote your energy, time, and efforts into a product idea you believe can be successful. This process is all about learning to recognize a product with potential — it is your top investment at this entrepreneurial stage.

If you decide to move forward with your product, it's time to stand firm and focus on the final product or service — and take it to the next level. Once you've made your decision, don't get distracted by others' efforts. It will always look "greener" on the other side of the fence — ignore the temptation to change your mind. Trust your decision-making skills, knowing that at this juncture, you have done extensive research and answered hard questions truthfully.

Focus

It's time to **FOCUS — *Follow One Course Until Successful***. Now that you have decided to run with the product, have created your first prototype, have heard from your peers, family, and advisors, and have completed some initial customer research, it's time to employ a laser focus on a targeted market and get real customers involved. An involved customer is your best investor. We want you to unleash a product from a solid launching pad, and you won't be ready until you have lined up several involved, sometimes demanding, and preferably very enthusiastic customers. These are your early product evangelists.

Remember, product ideas slowly evolve. They don't just turn on like light bulbs. This is especially true when you attempt developing, or pivoting, a product idea around real customer feedback. A demanding first customer can be your best catalyst to build a successful product.

OUR CUSTOMERS SEEM TO ALL HAVE DIFFERENT IDEAS OF WHAT IS BEST IN OUR PRODUCT..

I DID THE STATISTICS ON YOUR CUSTOMER FEEDBACK, AND THE MAJORITY PREFER THIS VERSION
LET'S MAKES THESE CHANGES AND TRY TO SELL SOME!"

Conduct Another Round of Customer Interviews

First, determine the best place to showcase your prototype, based upon your target demographic. You may present your prototype to random people in a specific town or on a specific street, or attend trade shows or farmers' markets.

Research: Spend about an hour a day for 4 days in different locations talking to customers. The goal is to talk to a minimum of 20 to 30 customers who fit your target. Don't waste time interviewing people who aren't your target customers. Everyone has opinions and suggestions. At this point, feedback from friends and family can distract you because they may not fit into your target market. Target customers are the only ones who count at this stage in your product evolution.

When you venture out to interview target customers, use a revised survey. Ask questions like:

- What is one thing you really like about my product?
- What is one thing you really don't like about my product?
- How would you improve this version?
- What new "must have" features does it need?
- How much would you pay for my product with these "must have" features?

Capture Testimonials

At this point in the interviewing process, it's okay to record responses. Have a video camera or iPad to capture customer testimonials — they are like gold when you pitch to investors later on. Video is the most desirable method for sharing your customers' feedback with potential investors or other potential customers. Of course, you must obtain customers' permission to video, or audiotape, their feedback. (You might consider having a release for them to sign, so you are free to use their words and image throughout the life of the product.)

When you return from the field, analyze the responses. The main goal involves integrating any improvement suggested from customers, wherever feasible. Look at what common complaints bubbled to the surface. Then consider the cost/benefit of changing your prototype to improve it based on customer feedback. Remember: Not every change is worth making immediately, as the cost may be prohibitive. When you feel you must make a key revision to your product but cannot afford it, simply make note of it. When you are ultimately ready to pitch your product, let your audience know which features you plan to incorporate in your revised prototype and how it will improve your product, according to overwhelming customer feedback.

Lather. Rinse. Repeat. Talking to customers at this stage is considered your second litmus test we referred to in Step 7. You need to repeat this process several times until you get your product concept "right" with willing and reliable buyers.

NOTES

13

Sell Prototypes

The ultimate test of your product idea is whether or not people will buy it. In this step, we will discuss how to sell an early version of your product. The emphasis here is on "selling," not "giving away," your product.

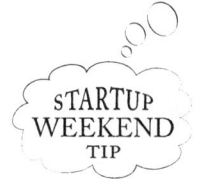

> **STARTUP WEEKEND TIP**
>
> IF YOU ARE UNABLE TO CREATE A SALEABLE PROTOTYPE BY SATURDAY AFTERNOON, SEE IF YOU CAN GET A PURCHASE ORDER FOR THE ADVANCE SALE OF ONE OR TWO UNITS.

Why Sell Now?

The best way to prove the concept of your product is by making a few local sales for money. Your goal is get at least one actual sale. The more sales in a short period of time you achieve, the better. Most of our students have been able to sell three to 10 units by the end of the semester. But one is good enough!

Just one sale is incredibly important, because it proves someone is willing to pay for your product. You can make deals with your first customers that help convince them to buy, such as guaranteed satisfaction or your money back. This takes the risk out of buying the first version of your product.

Selling locally allows you to maintain contact with your customers, in case the product needs returning. It also allows you to obtain feedback after they try it. (This is your third litmus test —getting feedback from real paying customers who will help you design your final product.) Obviously, local customers are easier to stay connected with during the first days and weeks they own your product. Your first customers will gladly tell you what they like and don't like about your product. Be sure to collect their contact information so you can follow up in the few days or weeks after your sale, in order to see how they like it. This early feedback can help you evolve a better and better product, so keep notes for the development of your next version.

How to Sell

Placement

Students often use Craigslist for free advertising. They also hang out at farmers' markets, place ads in the local paper and sell through events on and off campus — or even through retailers. For example, Garden on Wheelz™ was strategically placed at local nurseries. Not only did the nurseries help to sell units, but also, customers who bought the gardening bed also purchased soil, flowers and other supplies from the nurseries. Justin Connell had to work hard to carve out the relationship with the nurseries, but he did it. We encourage all of our students to get out there and talk to retailers as part of the program.

Sales Pitches that Emphasize USP

What do you say to customers to persuade them to buy your product? Before you approach customers, practice pitching your product, over and over, to family and friends, or classmates. Point out the best features of your product. Memorize your unique selling proposition and the characteristics that make your product stand out.

The Garden on Wheelz™ was an easy sell: It helps people continue their love of gardening as they grow older. It gives wheelchair-bound people access to the joy of gardening. It is eco-friendly, portable and simple to use and move around. And, in his research, Justin learned that retirement and assisted-living communities practice "horticulture therapy," so he links his product with this practice to sell more units.

Point out the most salient features of your product — the ones that will motivate customers to buy it. The NAK™ founder, Ty Blunt, found a niche by talking to customers. He learned that companies were looking for unique items to use at trade shows for giveaways. Most businesses at the trade shows were giving away the same items, and some companies wanted different "swag." One buyer gave Ty a purchase order for 10,000 units, to be branded with the company name for giveaways to clients and potential customers. Now, when Ty makes a sales call, he suggests use of his product as swag and sells the concept of having a unique giveaway at trade shows.

Price

In addition to working on your pitch, consider costs and how you will derive a realistic price for your first few sales. Review your customer validation surveys and the feedback you received when you asked: "What would you be willing to pay for my product?" What did customers say? Another consideration involves what your competition charges. You do not always have to be cheaper, especially if your product contains more features and delivers a higher quality product. However, it is best to be willing to give your early customers a super deal, with an explanation like this: "Our introductory price is $XX, which is 50% off our future retail price."

Make sure you figure in your current per-unit cost, and decide if you're willing to break even — or even lose money — rather than make a profit on your first few sales. We often suggest breaking even and letting buyers know you are selling the item at cost, which often attracts more customers. Of course, your longer-term plan involves lowering the manufacturing price, when you begin to mass-produce it. But for now, try to earn your costs back with your first few sales. If you planned to sell three and you sold 10, maybe your price is too low.

IN ORDER FOR US TO GET SOME INVESTOR INTEREST, WE REALLY NEED TO GET SOME SALES! ANY IDEAS?
WE COULD TRY SELLING TO MY PARENTS, AT LEAST THEY WOULD BE SUPPORTIVE

I'M NOT GOOD AT SELLING BUT I CAN TRACK SALES!
SALES IS A PIECE OF CAKE! HOW MANY DO YOU WANT ME TO SELL, AND MORE IMPORTANTLY, WHAT SHOULD BE THE PRICE OF OUR PRODUCT?

Depending upon your industry, a general rule of thumb is to double your per unit cost to derive a retail price. A good benchmark is to produce long-term gross profit margins between 30% and 40%. (Gross margin equals gross revenue less the costs of goods sold.)

Your Purpose Is to Get Early Fans of Your Product

We emphasize the importance of exchanging your product for money. It is what validates your concept — being able to demonstrate that people will pay money for what you are selling. But don't be greedy with your first sales. You want people to buy your product, love it, and talk about it to others. Your transaction should be a positive one, which means customers should love your price and willingly pay for it, knowing what a bargain they are getting. You may have to sell your first few "below cost," and that's okay. The point is, you sold them at a price that you may be able to match in the future with higher volume manufacturing, and thus, make a profit. Remember the point of this exercise is to prove to a potential investor that you have a product people will pay money for at a price that could eventually be profitable.

If you're extremely uncomfortable selling your product, pick the person on your team who can best make sales — the Expressive. Make use of the various business personality types and skills sets apparent on your team.

14

Know the Numbers

Start-up entrepreneurs can go overboard building multi-layer and multi-function spreadsheets that take a lot of time to conjure. They consider every possible variable the new company might encounter, which has little to no impact on investors. In this step, we will guide you through our method of presenting your financial model in the simplest yet most credible manner possible.

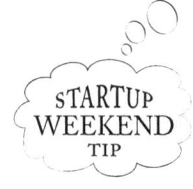

STARTUP WEEKEND TIP

THIS SIMPLE FINANCIAL METHOD IS IDEAL FOR YOUR SHORT WEEKEND ACTIVITIES. YOU WILL IMPRESS YOUR COLLEAGUES!

Faculty and coaches: If you are conducting a class, program, or Startup Weekend, we highly recommend you bring a financial expert into the room as a mentor to help students navigate the financial statements described below. We waited until this step to address the financial model, because by now students have a pretty solid grasp on pricing, including an estimated cost of manufacturing. They already know a lot of the required "numbers." Attempting to complete this forecasting and break-even analysis prior to this stage just frustrates students. Financial modeling tends to elicit grunts and groans from students, but at this stage, they are excited to put what they know on paper and begin predicting all of the money they will make!

If you are working the 20 steps in about 50 to 60 hours, you do not have time to roll out detailed financial models. You need to create only what is essential and to the point. There will be plenty of time later to refine and add variables, upon a potential investor's request. You will need to focus on four financial statements: Profit and Loss Statement, Balance Sheet, Break-Even Analysis, and Cash Flow 12-Month Forecast.

Think like a potential investor. What is the most important information he or she needs to size up your company both at this moment and in the next 12 months? We emphasize five key questions:

1. What are the up-front, non-recurring costs, namely: legal issues, engineering design, and licensing?
2. What are the projected, 12-months' spending amounts for the classic fixed costs, namely: rent, insurance, utilities, Internet service, and salaries?
3. What are the projected monthly sales for the next 12 months, namely: number of units sold and price per unit?
4. What are the projected, 12-months' spending amounts for the classic variable costs, namely: materials, shipping, phone charges, travel expenses, hourly labor, and taxes?
5. What are the 12-months' projected revenue amounts?

Profit & Loss

Work on a Profit and Loss sheet by creating a basic Excel spreadsheet, which shows your profit and loss numbers. In Appendix E, we have included a simple financial template that we use in the classroom. You can determine every expense with a little research. Call an insurance agent for a quote. Call a real estate broker for an estimate on rent per square foot in your area. Interview operators in your industry to project main expenses.

Revenue, on the other hand, involves a little more guesswork. You are not completely sure on price per unit (but you can make an educated guess based on your first sales). You aren't completely sure how many customers you will have and how many units you will sell in the first year, so you have to guess. You may have to make all of the sales during your first year by yourself — or with one salesperson on your team — so think this through as if you were mostly on your own. In the Garden on Wheelz™ example, Justin had to figure out how many nurseries would carry his product. With NAK™, Ty asked himself how many companies would likely place an order for 10,000 units per month. If you show a gradual and modest increase in sales each month based on your own potential efforts and your history of first sales, an investor will see that you have been conservative and realistic in your estimates. Investors (and judges) like conservative and realistic estimates.

At the bottom of your spreadsheet, you will show a cumulative profit or loss each month. Be very conservative in your projections, and don't be afraid to show a loss. This number helps you determine how much capital investment you will need in the first year. It is normal to end up in the loss column for the first 6 months.

Balance Sheet

The Balance Sheet gives a potential investor a snapshot of the financial condition of your company in any given moment of the first year. He or she wants to see the value of your assets, liabilities, and ownership equity. The Balance Sheet essentially shows an investor how you are financing your assets. Here is the simple accounting formula:

Assets = Liabilities + Equity

An asset is something valuable that you own and can generate revenue with — things like computers, product inventory, automobiles, and cash in the bank.

A liability is what the company is obliged to pay back — it is the "loan" you used to start the business.

Equity is the interest shareholders own in the company.

WHERE DID YOU GET ALL THESE NUMBERS?
FROM OUR SALES MANAGER, OF COURSE!

THESE FORECASTS ARE NOT BELIEVABLE. IT'S BETTER TO BE CONSERVATIVE AND CUT THESE NUMBERS IN HALF!
NO PROBLEM. WE KNOW THE OLD ADAGE THAT SAYS FIGURES DON'T LIE, BUT LIARS FIGURE

The sum of your assets and liabilities is always zero. If your Balance Sheet shows more assets than liabilities, you need to record owners' equity to bring the sum to zero. On the other hand, when you increase liabilities and don't adjust assets accordingly, your equity ownership decreases proportionately, in order to keep the sum of assets and liabilities at zero.

Break-Even Analysis

Determine your break-even month to see when you will begin to make a profit after you cover all of your expenses. This is an important threshold to cross — it's when spending equals revenue. However, you'll still have to assess how much you are "in the hole" when you reach break-even operations.

A more sophisticated way to calculate your break-even point is to calculate the number of units you need to sell to reach that break-even point where spending equals revenue. The question is, how many units do you need to sell each month to cover your expenses? For this calculation, you will need to differentiate your fixed costs from your variable costs.

Fixed costs are expenses that do not vary as unit sales increase, such as rent, insurance, utilities, and salaries. Fixed costs are expenses that are paid, regardless of the number of sales. They are sometimes referred to as overhead costs. Variable costs are expenses that rise or fall, depending upon the number of unit sales. These include things like shipping costs, manufacturing costs, labor, and materials.

To determine your break-even point, use the equation below:
- Break-even point = fixed costs / (unit selling price — variable costs). This calculation lets you know how many units you need to sell before you break even (cover your expenses) and begin to potentially make a profit.

Use your Break-Even Analysis only as a guidepost. It is simply a tool to get an idea of the relationship between your price point and number of units you need to sell to start making money. If you feel there is no way you can realistically sell that number of units in the time period based upon this formula, then you might need to revisit your pricing, or your expenses, and see what you can change.

Cash Flow Analysis

Your financial statements will include a Cash Flow 12-month Forecast, because you need to show potential investors that you will not run out of cash. After all, if you run out of money, your business will shut down.

In the forecast, you will assume you received investment dollars and enter that on a line item. If you recall, according to your Profit and Loss Statement, you probably will be running negative for the first 6 months. This is why you need to have a certain amount of cash in the bank to cover your expenses for the first year or longer.

Here's the formula:

Net Cash Flow = Cash Inflow - Cash Outflow

Cash flow is the money the company received using whatever means (operating, investing, etc.). Cash outflow is the cash the company paid for whatever reasons (primarily operating expenses). The spreadsheet should list the months across the top and your cash in-flow items along the left side, followed by your cash-outflow items. Appendix F contains a sample Cash Flow Forecast.

The point of this step is to demonstrate to potential investors that you have a handle on the current state of your business and the projected flow of business in the upcoming year. You become the expert on how much things will cost and how much time it will take to get this concept off the ground and turn a profit. There is no way around this task — you are it. If you have a team, look to your Analytic for help.

NOTES

15
Layout Marketing

If you can't plan it, you probably can't do it either. For start-ups, we encourage simple plans that you can easily change as the world teaches you what will work and what will not work. This step outlines the basics of a simple marketing plan.

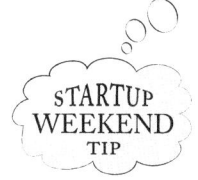

> **STARTUP WEEKEND TIP**
> INCORPORATE "WEDGIES" INTO YOUR SOCIAL MEDIA MARKETING PLAN FOR A QUICK AND EASY SURVEY TOOL THAT CAN BE COMPLETED BEFORE THE WEEKEND IS OVER!

Every investor always asks, "How will you market your product?" Formal marketing plans take into account numerous business factors, from historical financial performance to future growth plans and product diversification. You can earn an advanced degree in marketing, but for our limited purpose, we need only highlight the major components of a plan for advertising, branding and marketing your product in your first year.

Your choice of media and branding style depends entirely upon the target market you intend to reach. This step presents possibilities for you to formulate your own branding plan, based on your target market.

This is not the time to get overwhelmed, so recognize that creating your own brand can be fun!

Marketing Tools

Most companies employ a logo to brand their products. Branding places an authentic stamp on your product. Even though you are not a professional graphic designer, you can still come up with something basic to represent your product. This is also where another team member who possesses graphic or web-designing skills may come in handy. If no one fits the bill at the moment, you can wait until you create cash flow, and hire a professional to refine your logo later.

If you're doing it yourself, conduct a logo search on the Internet, and you will see thousands of other people's logos to inspire you. As you create your logo, take into account the age group and style of your target customers — are they young and hip or older and more conservative? Let the personality of your target market drive you in deciding the style and feel of your logo.

In addition to a logo, create a tag line (branding slogan). It should be simple, short, and to the point so that it describes your product or service in about six words.

Be Consistent

Once you have established these marketing tools, remain consistent with your branding. Every piece of communication from here on out should look and feel the same. Anything you disseminate to people about your business should contain your logo, web address and contact information. Use your logo and tag line on business cards, print advertisements, and any Internet presence. You can design and order business cards online inexpensively. For just $15, you can buy 500 business cards on sites like nextdayflyers.com or vistaprint.com. This is how you begin to brand your product, your company and yourself and gradually become familiar to the public. It has to be consistent, every time.

One of our student teams created a business called Craigfetch™. Their idea was to deliver anything for sale on Craigslist. Their tag line is: "We Fetch So You Don't Have To." They have become a popular delivery service for large item retrieval and small deliveries. Their logo, a dog chewing a couch, has a retro feel that appeals to both young and older people. Everywhere you find their service, you see their logo. They have done an excellent job with branding and have been consistent from the start. The partners carry business cards and coupons everywhere they go and pass them around to anyone they see. Every marketing piece they created has the same look and feel, and it is becoming a recognizable brand.

Learn from our students. Wherever you go, carry your business cards and talk about your business. Start locally as word of mouth travels fast, especially in small towns. It is important to share your own anecdotal stories about your product and how you started it. In addition, use specific stories from your customers that you have been collecting and tell others about their experience with your product or service. People like hearing stories — and passing them along. And, people believe what their friends tell them.

Social Media

Social media is a necessity when marketing your company, no matter what type of business you create. The single most important reason to take advantage of social media marketing is that you can potentially reach hundreds of millions of people *for free*. Like word of mouth, social media creates a buzz. Last we checked, Facebook had 1.1 billion active users per month. However, always consider your target audience. Will much older people who want to take up gardening again be on Facebook? Maybe some will, but most may not know how to navigate social media. Will students who need help moving a couch be on Facebook? Yes!

Either way, keep up with social media changes, and take advantage of all channels that apply to your target — Twitter, Facebook, Linkedin, Instagram, Pinterest and so on. Some new media always pops up. If

IF YOU CAN'T PLAN IT, YOU CAN'T DO IT.
WE NEED A REALISTIC MARKETING PLAN TODAY - NO FRILLS, FOCUSED, AND SPARTAN!
PUSHING THE TEAM TOO HARD TO ACHIEVE THE IMPOSSIBLE DOESN'T MAKE US FEEL GOOD

IF YOU CAN'T PLAN IT, YOU CAN'T DO IT.
LET'S KEEP IT SIMPLE, I'LL BUILD US A UNIQUE WEBSITE, AND THE CUSTOMERS WILL COME IN DROVES!
LET'S TAKE FULL ADVANTAGE OF SOCIAL MEDIA, AND I CAN SET UP A SELLER'S ACCOUNT ON AMAZON

you're unfamiliar with social media, there are plenty of books about the platforms for your business; we highly recommend *The 36-Hour Course to Online Marketing* by Lorrie Thomas. Of course, your brand and the need to be consistent apply to all social media as well. When you build a Facebook page, make sure it looks and feels like your brand.

As you make sales, consider paid online advertising sites — social marketing sites like Groupon or Living Social may be a good choice for advertising once you develop a solid marketing budget. Facebook ads also are cheap, and you can focus your ads on a specific target audience.

Build Your Own Temporary Website

Though it may seem daunting, building your own website isn't that difficult if you choose one of the various options that caters to small businesses. You don't even need programming skills. You can also use a number of free blog-based platforms to build your own website. We like Google's Blogger. It isn't as robust and flexible as WordPress, but if you are an inexperienced first-timer on your own, it offers a simple and easy way to learn quickly.

You can purchase a URL for $10 or less from a number of sites like GoDaddy or Register.com and use their free forwarding service to point to the blog-based site you have built to your official URL. This technique legitimizes your first site — you have a real URL (not a blog address) with a page or two showcasing your product.

When you first build the site, make it informational only, with one or two pages. On Blogger, you can turn off the blog tools and create up to 10 tabs across the top to make the site look more like web pages, as opposed to a blog. Owning a web page — however basic — adds to your credibility and helps strengthen your brand. You can upgrade and/or professionally spruce it up later, when you can afford it.

Traditional Advertising & Networking

Once you've built an online presence, determine whether or not a traditional advertising plan is right for you. But beware: Print ads are usually expensive and are very target-customer dependent. Baby Boomers (born from 1946 to 1964) are more likely to see this form of advertising because they still buy newspapers.

Also consider putting out a press release. Journalists look for unique stories, and if yours fits their angle and target audience, you can build your own buzz with a bang-up press release about the "launch" of your product or service. It's free to submit press releases, though you may want to get help writing one, as journalists are used to a particular style and level of professionalism. The Internet offers sample press releases, which can help you write your own release. Add photos of your product to make it easier for reporters to "see" the entire picture. Most often, your product will fit into the business section, but wherever it fits, your best chance for obtaining interest involves making personal contact with reporters. Email the press releases to a number of newspapers, especially local ones where you live. Some will simply print your release as written, and, if you're lucky, reporters will contact you for a more robust story.

You may also find that tradeshows enable you to increase public awareness. Determine whether your industry thrives on tradeshows, and research which ones perfectly match your product. Be very selective about which ones to attend, as tradeshows are expensive and require travel. They're usually not warranted in the early stage for a start-up, but you should know the names and dates of the tradeshows you would like to attend as your product matures.

Networking events usually are more practical to attend than tradeshows. If the events are free, you have no excuse to miss this opportunity. They can be a great place to meet contacts that could help you in the future. However, when choosing networking events, verify that potential investors, mentors or your target customers frequent the ones you choose. At the events, pass out business cards, flyers, and surveys — whatever you have that showcases your business. Also collect business cards from other attendees. Networking is a two-way street — you talk about yourself and your product, and they talk about their products. The next day, follow up with people you think may be helpful in the future, and make sure to maintain an ongoing contact list so that you can follow-up when appropriate.

Placement

Now that you have your sales' pitch down, you are advertising on social media, have a website and other marketing tools up and running, it may be time to approach retail stores, in order to test your product — if you haven't already. Make an appointment with store owners or managers and ask if they will accept your product on "consignment." Offer to represent your product during high-volume hours at the stores. Also, make sure the stores' buyers can easily order from you — and that you can follow through with volume.

These suggestions are by no means exhaustive, but hopefully you have enough ideas to help create your first mini-marketing plan and start creating materials that represent your brand.

16

Outline Operations

The process of creating an operational plan forces an entrepreneur to think through all of the critical aspects of a new business — activities like accounting, billing, and order fulfillment. Typically, the challenge is how to do all these activities with a very limited staff, or no staff at all. This step guides you through the questions you need to answer, and offers tips for a smooth first year.

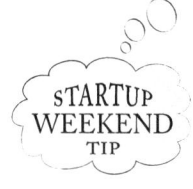

> **STARTUP WEEKEND TIP**
>
> OPERATIONS CAN ENCOMPASS SO MANY MOVING PARTS. STAY FOCUSED ON DAY-TO-DAY OPERATIONS THAT WILL AFFECT THE BUSINESS OVER THE NEXT 12 MONTHS.

We are not going to cover high-level expert operations in this step. Once a company reaches a certain level of sales (in the millions) and it begins to grow exponentially, an operations strategy becomes more of a central focus. Here, we just need to get through the next 12 months of your start-up. Operations generally address the necessary processes, from production through sales. Operations are also concerned with the physical and technical functions.

GETTING OUR PRODUCT MANUFACTURED, BOXED, AND STORED TO MEET EXISTING SALES DEMAND WILL BE NO JOKE!
Flowchart
Start
Process step 1
Decision?
Choice 2
Choice 1
Process step 2
A
WE HAVE TALENTED PEOPLE. CAN WE ENCOURAGE SOME OVERTIME AND BONUSES?

OUR MARGINS ARE SO SLIM. I WOULD BE WORRIED TO ADD MORE TO THE BOTTOM-LINE COSTS. DO YOU HAVE ANY OTHER IDEAS?
Flowchart
Start
Process step 1
Decision?
Choice 2
Choice 1
Process step 2
A
IN MY HUMAN RESOURCE EXPERIENCE, EMPLOYEES CAN BE VERY MOTIVATED WITH A PROFIT SHARING PLAN. A WIN-WIN FOR EVERYBODY!

For our purposes, we want to focus on the microcosm of day-to-day sales, and leave the long view to the experts. The overarching concept here involves convincing a potential investor that you are planning ahead and can project the near-term needs. As you determine your actual need by considering the factors below, you can estimate the potential cost of your near-future growth and include that cost in your financials.

Point of Sales (POS) Systems

To start, you need to determine how you will receive money from the sales you make. In other words, what kind of merchant service provider will you use? If you are capturing credit card sales, you need a mechanism for doing so. Every company that provides this service takes a cut from your sales — in the form of a "per transaction" fee, a percentage of sales, or both. The percentage of sales can run anywhere from 1% to 4% or more, depending on your service provider.

There are so many service providers — and so many options available from providers. Even Costco offers a merchant system. Check with your bank as a starting point to see what it offers. The key is to find the best provider for your purpose, at the best cost. You will probably have to sign a 1- or 2-year contract to obtain the best rates. Still, it's a good idea to compare rates every year to ensure you are getting the lowest rates.

Once you choose a provider, you will need some type of hardware, called a POS system, to capture credit card swipes. You can use gadgets that work with your smartphone, or you can purchase a traditional swipe system. Either way, the hardware needs to link to your bank or PayPal account so that you actually receive the funds. Again, spend some time researching your options to find the best price and the most convenient system for your purposes. Even if you only accept online payments, you still need to seriously research what companies offer the best e-commerce services and packages, as well as the best customer service. Look into their reputation — which will ensure you can make sales online and render it easy for your customers? We know a lot of business owners that use Google Checkout, PayPal, and Intuit products.

And, after you choose a POS provider, your work isn't quite finished. You will need to build an e-commerce interface on your website. Perhaps find a competent friend or low-cost web designer to do the job.

Bookkeeping & Payroll Services

You'll need to decide how to handle invoicing, accounting, and billing. We like QuickBooks for start-ups and small business, but you can use any software you prefer to keep track of your finances. Accounting software is a minimal investment that pays huge dividends later. It helps keep your customers — plus your invoicing, bills, and bank accounts — in order, in a very user-friendly way, and will pay dividends at tax time with an easy reports platform. QuickBooks is currently pushing its online services, which is extremely convenient and accessible anywhere, but other good online accounting software services exist, as well. Excel is a viable option to keep track of your finances if you know Excel and how to use formulas.

We recommend holding off on hiring employees as long as you possibly can. When payroll enters the picture, things become a little complicated, because any software you choose needs to provide payroll capability. You will not be able to afford a fancy payroll service until much later (such as ADP). In addition, payroll is expensive for a start-up. The minute you hire an employee, your company is on the hook for payroll taxes and company contributions such as Medicare and Social Security. Detailed tracking of all of the taxes and payroll expenses is critical to avoiding penalties, and handling deadlines can become an expensive requirement.

The next question is: Should you hire a bookkeeper? Our vote is no — at least not yet. The best way to fully understand your business is to keep track of your own bills and accounting. Sure, you will need an accountant at tax time, but for your first year, track your own finances and make it a priority to learn a simple accounting software package so you do it right. You need to enter every expense and categorize it. If you make a mistake categorizing an expense, your accountant can clean it up at the end of the fiscal year. For now, take control and do it yourself with an eye for detail. Wait until you can afford the luxury of a bookkeeper.

Manufacturing

Now, concerning the manufacturing side: How you are going to handle production over the next 12 months? Your garage can only accommodate a limited amount of manufacturing and inventory storage. At some point, you will need to move to the next level as the volume of sales increase and investors and prospective clients ask questions about your location. Basically, you'll need to consider outsourcing. Research manufacturing companies in your industry. Are any local so that you can visit and monitor them, or is local too expensive? If so, perhaps you can utilize local resources for a few months and then move production to a different location.

Gather quotes from as many U.S. manufacturers as you can in order to gauge cost as you proceed to higher volumes. Unfortunately, manufacturing is often cheapest overseas, in countries like China and Thailand, but the logistics of foreign manufacturing can be overwhelming during your first year. If you choose this route, ensure you have the right contacts and mentors to help you navigate this decision and do it right. Manufacturing in the U.S. vs. abroad can affect not only your bottom line, but also your reputation with customers.

Local resources can help you make such decisions. The local Small Business Development Center (SBDC) in our area has international manufacturing experts and counselors who travel frequently to China and speak Mandarin, and have personal contacts on the ground. They offer their advice at no cost. SBDC's exist nationwide to help you.

As you begin to manufacture goods, determine how much inventory you need on hand, and decide where you will store it. As your sales volume grows, you may need a warehouse, in order to ensure you can meet orders without running out and going on backorder.

Research: We recommend spending about 4 hours researching all of the above, to help you lay out your 12-month operations summary.

Licenses and Permits: Once you are engaged in the sale of goods, you will likely need to obtain a business license or permit in your local city. Every city, county and state has different requirements. Research the government websites in your city, county and state to determine the legal requirements. In addition, you may need a fictitious business name statement, or obtain a Federal Tax ID. Before you can hire an employee, you need to file papers with the government and begin paying taxes to the government within the first 3 months. Make sure you get the help you need from a mentor or SBDC consultant to ensure you are complying with all federal, state, county and city laws in your area.

NOTES

Outline Operations

17
Chart Distribution

Making the right choices for sales and distribution is a key element of your business model. You must be able to show investors how you plan to reach your market and that you know approximately how much it will cost. They want to know things like: Will you use a distribution company? Will you sell online and offline? Will you sell through retail or wholesale? Will you export? This step helps you identify potential issues to get you started with research and an initial plan.

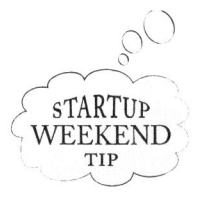

> **STARTUP WEEKEND TIP**
>
> SALES AND DISTRIBUTION CHANNELS ARE USUALLY ADDRESSED AFTER THE WEEKEND AND FURTHER DOWN THE PRODUCT DEVELOPMENT ROAD. THIS STEP WILL HELP YOU ANTICIPATE WHAT'S NEXT.

Michael Houlihan, co-founder of Barefoot Wines, told the Scheinfeld Center that every company has only two departments: Sales, and Sales Support. As you move into selling at higher volumes, you can no longer remain connected to every customer. Your sales force becomes your direct link to the customers. They become the people who represent you and your brand. This step reviews points to help you develop a plan that best serves you, your product, your brand, and your customers.

Plan for a Sales Team

At this early stage, you probably don't need a sales team. You and your early founding team are going to be "it." But it's wise to plan for growth — and help — in the next 6 months or so. We suggest identifying two or three other people who can assist you with sales in the upcoming months, be it family members, friends, or new partners. These sales people will help generate leads through cold calls, and follow-up with potential buyers. Begin to target those kinds of decision makers now.

Consider how you will pay your sales team. Several options exist, including: commission only, hourly or salary plus commission, and/or incentives. It's all negotiable, but you should have a preference to use as a starting point. Some entities sign up resellers that either work solely on commission, or are allocated a baseline monthly stipend that is considered an advance against commissions. This could be less expensive than a full-time hire. Note that resellers often represent other businesses at the same time they represent you, so be sure to address any conflict or competing issues.

Consider what kind of sales tactics or strategies you will use. Will you provide demonstrations? Create a pilot project for customers to "try before they buy?"

Customer Service

By the time you hire a sales force, you should be able to describe your marketing philosophy and customer service plan and articulate this to your sales team. Define your specific practices of rendering quality customer service. Figure out how you, or another specific person on your team, will connect with customers after sales. In other words, how will you collect customers' contact information, and how will you devise an easy way to receive customer feedback, both good and bad. Some useful options are toll-free numbers, email contacts, and websites with frequently asked questions (FAQs) and forms to complete. Whatever route you choose, it's imperative to know how you will receive complaints and how you will respond to them rapidly. Also determine specifics about your return policy and whether or not you will offer product guarantees or warranties for at least a minimal period of time.

Payment Terms

In terms of payment, decide if customers will pay in advance, or if you'll offer credit terms. If you choose the latter, what are the credit terms? Will you impose penalties for late payment? If you choose the former, and the business offers a service, it could be beneficial to offer discounts to clients that pay up front for longer commitments.

Distribution

Although you may not think of it this way, distribution is actually part of your customer service planning. How you deliver your product to your customer affects your reputation and your customers' satisfaction.

The type of distribution (direct or in stages, to the consumer) depends largely upon the industry you occupy. It also answers the question of how your customers receive products — and who helps deliver it all. Barefoot Wine employed brokers, and distribution companies to transport pallets of wine to its large retailers, and then the retailers sold bottles of wine to customers. Barefoot Wine's distribution system helped it become the number one selling wine in the U.S. The founders didn't simply hire a distribution company. They talked to the forklift operators and listened to common delivery problems, then decided how to proceed.

One important aspect of distribution involves regulatory compliance issues, in terms of packaging and labeling for your product. Research what is required in your industry before you make any delivery promises.

Depending upon the size of your product, it may be necessary to ship it in pieces, obliging customers to assemble the product. Don't fret over this too much. Americans are quite accustomed to self-service when it comes to assembling new products. Of course, you must carefully think this process through, in order to make assembly as easy as possible for the customer.

142 The Practical Guide to a Rapid Start-up

As you put your distribution plan together, research various distribution systems, taking note of cost, delivery terms and timing. Ensure your product can be shipped easily, especially if you're depending on Internet sales, which requires simple and inexpensive shipping. The more shippable your product, the better it is. Most rapid start-ups prove their products locally, and then open a "sellers" account on eBay, or other online retailers — or personal websites. Though this opens you to nationwide — and even worldwide — sales, we don't recommend this step while you're still "evolving" your product. E-commerce is a stage-two selling strategy.

Once you decide on your distribution method, don't rest on your laurels. Distribution methods continue to evolve. Stay current on the latest and greatest systems. Outline all of the possible distribution systems, people, technologies, and companies you could access to deliver your product to consumers, either directly or indirectly — and save it for future reference.

Research: We recommend about 4 hours to research distribution channels and hone in on a couple of specific distributors to talk to about your company's future plan and costs.

(Left to right) Founders AJ Forsythe and Anthony Martin

This company is an example of providing a solution to a pain that is simple, flexible, reasonably priced, and scalable.

The Founders

AJ Forsythe – founded iCracked in 2010 while attending the California Polytechnic University (Cal Poly) in San Luis Obispo after breaking his iPhone a few too many times. After graduating from Cal Poly and teaming up with Anthony Martin, he started growing iCracked into the what is today the world's largest, on-demand repair and buyback network for iOS devices with over 400 elite, mobile iTechs nationwide and abroad.

Anthony Martin – Attended the University of California at Santa Barbara (UCSB) to play baseball. Anthony is the Chief Strategy Officer in charge of creating new and innovative ways for iCracked to serve the iOS ecosystem throughout the lifecycle of a device.

Mission Statement > iCracked is committed to being the world's preeminent authority on Smartphone repair by creating an extensive network of elite, mobile iTechs to service customers where and when they need it.

Company Growth > The company has grown to over 400+ iTechs while adding 50 to 70 new iTechs a month. Their revenues have grown from $2MM in 2012 to over $10MM in 2013. Their core team has grown from the 3 in 2010 to 30 in 2013.

Business Model >

1. On-Demand Repair: A customer will visit the company's site to request a dispatch to repair their iPhone, iPod or iPad. An iTech will claim the dispatch within 60 seconds and set up a time and place to perform the repair that is most convenient for the customer. Most repairs can be done in under an hour. This is the best option to get your device repaired quickly and locally.
2. Do-It-Yourself Repair: iCracked sells DIY kits containing a replacement screen/LCD/Digitizer as well as all the tools needed and proprietary flow chart. Plus, they have comprehensive repair videos on YouTube.
3. Mail-In Repair: For those customers that don't have an iTech in their area and aren't up to performing a DIY repair, they offer mail-in repair services.

Chart Distribution

18

Consider Investment

Every start-up begins cash starved, so prepare to draw from the "well" several times as you develop your business. There is even a term for how fast start-ups use investors' money, and it is called the "burn rate." Regardless of your new product or service, knowing how and when to seek capital investment is critical. In this step, you will learn about the two most relevant sources of capital: angel investors and venture capital.

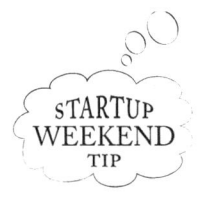

> **STARTUP WEEKEND TIP**
>
> ONE OF THE BENEFITS OF THE WEEKEND IS ALL THE BUZZ IN ADVANCE AND THE NUMEROUS INVITATIONS THAT GO OUT. HOPEFULLY, YOU FIND A GOOD POOL OF POTENTIAL INVESTORS THERE — BUT DON'T STOP WHEN THE STARTUP WEEKEND ENDS. CONTINUE TO PITCH IN AS MANY VENUES AS POSSIBLE.

Your master plan is to "bootstrap." This word is derived from an early American metaphor of pulling yourself over the fence by your bootstraps — an impossible task. We use the term to denote building your business without outside investment, which is not an impossible task. Put everything in it you can — your skills and expertise, your research, your teamwork, and your own money, until you develop a proven concept and saleable prototype. Some of our teams have continued without outside funding, but those businesses won't scale. Some of our teams didn't pursue their concepts past the classroom. Several students successfully pursued investment and are still going and growing.

What You Want in an Investor

At some point, you need to consider bringing in investors to help propel your business to the next level, if you want to scale and grow to attract a corporate buyer. (We discuss exit strategies in more detail in the last step).

Accepting capital from others is tricky business. You must be familiar with various types of investment schemes and terminology. But more importantly, you must understand that once you accept investment from someone, it's like a marriage — and it can be good or bad. You can feel like your investment partner supports you wholeheartedly throughout your growth phases, or you can feel like you are trapped and suffocating.

Entrepreneurs often look at investing backwards. They desperately need money, and they feel fortunate when anyone wants to invest, so they seal a deal without properly investigating who, or what, they are dealing with. Rather than coming from a desperate position, think of it this way: The investor must qualify for the "investment position" *you* have open. Investing in start-ups is considered "high risk" because there is no guarantee investors will ever see their money again. But the potential returns are enormous and as such, many investors are willing to take that risk.

To put potential investment into proper perspective, you are now convinced that you can make a profit with your concept and you have a plan ready to put into action. How many viable investments are out there for the typical investor? Very few attractive options exist given the current economic climate. Banks yield next to nothing on money-market accounts and CDs, bonds are at historical lows, the stock market is unstable, and the real estate market can reset at any time. You and your idea represent risk, but potentially a phenomenal opportunity. **No other opportu-**

nity can yield a greater rate of wealth acquisition than an investment in a small company before it becomes successful. While it is important to remain realistic, keep this in mind as you meet and negotiate with potential investors.

Optimally, you need an investor who is also an expert advisor either in subject matter or sales channels. Investors should excel in the industry or be closely connected to big buyers in your industry. It's a red flag to you if someone wants to invest in your catering business but doesn't have any food retail experience or connections. Of course, their lack of experience isn't always a deal breaker — you should just look into partnering with them with greater caution and only after careful investigation and research.

Another red flag for you involves investors' unwillingness to give you the money they promise. You might think this an obvious point to make, but be wary of people who ask you to pay them. This happens! Investors come in all shapes and sizes — and with different moral compasses. Investors genuinely interested in your success will be wealthy enough to risk large investment dollars to help you attain the next level. They never will ask you to pay them until it's time to collect their agreed upon return on investment.

Any investor should have a track record of successful investing. He or she should generally possess wealth and be a "qualified" or "accredited" investor with the proper monetary ratios to take on the risk of "betting on" your business. The funds the investor spends should be discretionary, meaning he or she can lose it all, and such a loss would not create financial hardship.

In addition to understanding financial models (or providing an expert to help you spend appropriately along the way), investors should have a positive and exciting attitude about what you are doing. Investors can be your champions to motivate you, and perhaps even mentor you or otherwise involve themselves in the company.

SALES ARE SLOWING DUE TO OUR LACK OF CAPITAL FOR INFRASTRUCTURE!
BUT WE HAVE PROVEN THAT CUSTOMERS LOVE OUR PRODUCT!

WE NEED MORE MONEY TO KEEP OUR MOMENTUM. CAN YOU HELP ME PUT TOGETHER A PITCH TO INVESTORS?
OF COURSE! AND, I CAN RESEARCH ANGEL INVESTORS THAT MIGHT BE INTERESTED

However, mentors can sometimes disguise themselves as investors and ask for coaching fees. You do not have the luxury to pay anyone for business advice right now. Take advantage of your mentor team and free or low-cost government resources in the community (e.g., SBDC and SCORE).

> *Some people may approach you and offer to represent you to other investors for a "finder's fee." Make sure you understand the implications in this scenario. Finder's fees are only allowable in the event the agency wanting to represent you is a registered SEC broker. It can be illegal to pay finder's fees in an investment deal without the "finder" possessing the proper credentials. Most lay people who want to introduce you to someone they know ask for finder's fees without knowing this is a legal issue. There are legitimate and useful finder options; just be sure to protect your interests by negotiating specific performance metrics and have a contract in advance.*

What an Investor Wants in You

On the other side of the coin, investors will look for certain qualities in you and your company.

If an investor is on the right track, he or she will only be interested in certain industries close to his or her heart — either from personal experience or personal passion. An investor wants to finance something he or she feels connected to and knows a lot about, in terms of type of industry. Investors need to agree on your vision. They want to know where you're spending their money. They will analyze how much you plan to pay yourself and how your spending will help you reach certain milestones.

They will review your history of performance in school, on the job, and in this (or past) business venture. They want to ensure you have "skin in the game" and are willing to go the extra mile to make your business work. They want to see how much passion and dedication you have to make this happen. Investors often demand a positive "can do" attitude. Many investors also want to know what you will do with your money if you become successful, so be prepared to answer this question. In addition, they want to invest in something free of legal issues and ownership issues.

> *A note on investor activity: Convincing someone to invest in your company is very difficult, and it only gets harder as the economy lags or remains mercurial. Getting in front of investors willing to hear your pitch is also difficult. We recommend pitching in as many venues and competitions as possible to cast a wide net over investment activity and investor gatherings. Our local community is small, and large investment dollars often come from outside the community. There is no magic answer to finding the right audience, but persistence is the key. Your task is to spread the word about your idea in as many places as possible. (We discuss this in more detail in the next step on pitching.)*

Angel Investors

The origin of the term "angel investing" derives from theater enthusiasts who helped launch Off-Broadway plays and musicals. These were very high-risk opportunities, but the "angels" loved the theater and enjoyed the fruits of their investments by being able to attend these plays and musicals as often as they liked and possibly watching their investments grow and produce returns many times over.

Angel investors are usually quite wealthy and very well connected in certain industries where they have been involved, either through their own business or previous investments. They usually invest personal money, with very little constraints. It's up to you and the angel investor to come up with mutually agreeable terms. They generally prefer simple terms without a lot of legal involvement. They may or may not want to be involved hands-on but will generally guide and mentor you if you need it. Angel investors often negotiate to be appointed to your board of directors so they can influence your plans and progress.

Some potential angel investors for you may include: your parents, aunts or uncles, friends of the family, someone in an audience who hears your pitch, a customer, and an unexpected benefactor. In fact, a first customer who really needs your "would-be" product may very well consider paying you to design your product with his or her help. A knowledgeable first customer sometimes can be your best investor.

Investment Rounds

Money is invested in "rounds." You can refer to your first round as the "friends and family" one (usually under $50,000). Your second round could be the "angel" round (roughly $50,000 to $500,000). Then you move to larger investment rounds, which may require venture capital (VC), discussed below.

Most experts agree that you should accept angel money if you find the right investor. Overall, it's a lot less complicated than VC investments. The equity exchanged for a VC investment often does not allow you to maintain significant ownership, and with angel investors, you end up dealing with fewer individuals (usually less than 10 and often just one or two) who seem to care about you, rather than a firm that is mostly interested — and appropriately so — in the bottom line.

For example, Garden on Wheelz™ founder Justin Connell connected with his investor by pitching at the Clean Business Investment Summit at UCSB in Santa Barbara. A friend of a friend heard his pitch and set him up with a potential investor. His angel investor maintains connections to chains of assisted living centers around the country. So far, Justin has received $450,000 in investments, with a company valuation of $2 million. Throughout the process, Justin has made some smart decisions in retaining a majority ownership interest. He's using his attained investments for research and development, as well as expanding sales channels and generating leads.

Almost all companies budget money for research and development (R&D), and this includes funds for: developing new products, improving products, creating better manufacturing techniques for existing products, and programming software. In Justin's case, he dedicated some of his investment dollars toward his final prototype iteration. He ended up incorporating many features of his original prototype but significantly changed the materials (to recycled rubber), and added adjustable legs and other features customers asked for.

Venture Capital

As we mentioned, money is invested in "rounds." When you reach the stage of requiring investment in the millions, you must consider venture capital. We will not go into major detail here, but we want you to be aware of the basic differences between angel investing and venture capital.

Venture capital firms invest in large dollar amounts (often a minimum of $3 million). These firms conduct a tremendous amount of research, called "due diligence." They usually employ a complex in-house process, which takes a long time because as the investment dollar amount increases so, too, does the risk. As a result of the high dollar amount, venture firms may require a large commitment in equity. They also often require your company to form a board of directors, upon which at least one member of the venture firm will maintain a board seat.

A Word on Crowdfunding: These days, crowdfunding can be a serious consideration for small start-ups. Crowdfunding is a way to raise money on the Internet with a pool of investors — it's made up of a crowd of people that invest in companies in exchange for gifts, recognition, and, now, equity. Recently, the Securities & Exchange Commission approved a new rule [506c)] that lifts some of the restrictions on crowdfunding, paving the way for companies to advertise to the public that they are raising capital in exchange for equity and allowing a limited number of investors to be non-accredited. (To learn more, visit: http://www.sec.gov/news/press/2013/2013-124-item1.htm and http://www.forbes.com/sites/chancebarnett/2013/07/19/sec-finally-moves-on-equity-crowdfunding-phase-1/)

There are pros and cons to crowdfunding. The most notable risk is that you must manage and report to a crowd of investors that you don't know, which can backfire. There are numerous crowdfunding sites cropping up every day, with various applications and industry specializations. We advise researching extensively before jumping in and starting a crowdfunding campaign. (Learn more at: http://www.inc.com/magazine/201306/ eric-markowitz/how-to-choose-a-crowdfunder.html)

*A note on "Splitting the Pie": There is an excellent article on how funding works at fundersandfounders.com (How Funding Works: Splitting the Equity Pie with Investors). The authors' point is this: At first you own 100% of a very small pie worth, say, $100,000. But as you start splitting up the pie and giving away equity ownership in exchange for investments, the pie grows bigger and bigger (if done properly). So at the end of the road, you may only own 15% of the pie, but the pie is now worth $20 million and your "mere" 15% is worth $3 million. Having said that, it is crucial you educate yourself on concepts like **dilution, pre-money valuation, stock options, bridge notes, discounts,** and **warrants** before you reach the investment point in your company.*

19

Pitch, Pitch, Pitch

A great pitch is short, simple to understand, factual, and delivered in a credible, authentic, and exciting way. In this step, we will help you prepare a great, stand-out pitch.

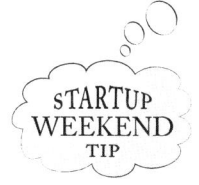

> **STARTUP WEEKEND TIP**
>
> FOR YOUR FIRST PITCH, YOU HAVE ONLY 60 SECONDS! IF YOU ARE UNABLE TO GRAB ATTENTION AND MAKE YOUR POINT IMMEDIATELY, VOTERS WON'T CHOOSE YOUR IDEA.

Pitching is an art form, which you can learn to do with pride and confidence. The best pitches showcase your unique, authentic voice and reveal your personality and passion about what you are trying to sell. If you can't convey your excitement and passion, no one else is going to get excited about it.

Some great pitches employ attention-grabbing gimmicks. For example, Richard Branson successfully used a magic trick! He garnered a $5 million discount on an Airbus to start up Virgin Airlines when he convinced the CEO and the Airbus team that he had hypnotized the CEO, who then handed over his watch to Branson (though it was only sleight of hand). We suggest you just be yourself, be passionate and exuberant, and rev up the audience about your new venture.

GUY KAWASAKI'S
10-20-30 RULE
THESE SLIDES ARE TERRIBLE AND THE PITCH IS TOO LONG! NO INVESTOR WILL LISTEN TO THIS!
WE HAVE GREAT FEEDBACK FROM POTENTIAL CUSTOMERS, SO WE SHOULD INCLUDE THAT!

GUY KAWASAKI'S
10-20-30 RULE
I CAN MAKE A CHART SHOWING OUR NUMBERS
LET ME PRACTICE A 10-MINUTE PITCH AND SHOW YOU GUYS TOMORROW

How to Deliver Great Pitches

When pitching at a formal event or contest, read the event's rules and follow them. Rules vary, from the order of topics to cover to the number of slides in your deck. Change your pitch according to the regulations for each venue.

As you prepare your content, remember that the horse must come out of the gate immediately! A general rule of thumb is to begin your pitch by describing the problem, and follow it up with your solution. You need to ensure the audience understands your product or service within the first 60 seconds — including what pain it solves. One of the biggest mistakes you can make is to pitch for 5 minutes or so, without clearly explaining your product or service. Audiences need to know up front what your idea is so they can process the rest of the information you share, as it applies to your idea. Most pitches last about 10 minutes (give or take a couple). Highlight the most important points of your idea, and devote about 1 minute to each of the following 11 topics:

1. What's the problem?
2. What's your unique solution?
3. How are you going to make money doing it?
4. What are your financial projections for the next 12 months?
5. How do you produce the product and deliver it to customers?
6. How will you raise awareness and market it to your customers?
7. Who is your competition, and how can you beat them?
8. Why is your idea so great? What is your USP?
9. What have you done so far (product development, prototypes, sales)?
10. Who are your mentors? How can your mentors/partners help catapult your business to the next level? What kinds of skills do you need to round out your team?
11. How much money do you need, and how do you plan on spending it?

Slide Deck & Props

PowerPoint slides often help convey your business idea well. We feel that slides are best utilized when employed as a visual complement to your words to further illustrate what you are saying, as opposed to simply mimicking your words (typed on a slide).

We suggest creating one slide for each of the 11 topics you address. Most competitions limit slides to 10 or 12 and do not allow embedded slides. If you insist on using words in your slides, use nothing smaller than a 30-point font.[1] Design your slides more like "cue" cards than text. Figure out how you can "show" your point to the audience in a way that communicates your message and prompts you to expand on it. Examples of ways to use visuals, rather than words, include using pictures of your prototypes and teammates, pictures of your logo, pictures of your customers, graphs of your financials, and charts depicting your manufacturing growth process. Try to create a sense of excitement. Review some of Steve Jobs' famous presentations online to see how, with very few words, he generates tremendous excitement. Pitching is a performance, but with a key objective in mind — to identify the right types of partners.

Highlighting your presentation with a compelling video clip can positively impact your audience's experience, but only use video when it adds to a visual understanding. When utilized properly, it's like a picture — worth a thousand words, because seeing is believing. Video also provides an entertainment factor. People want to be wowed by all the labor you've put into this. Show them how hard you've worked to get here! Of course, test your video on the equipment at the venue before your pitch. Come up with a contingency plan in case the video clip doesn't work, because it happens — often. If it does, simply move onto the next slide or point, as if you planned it that way.

---

[1] The now ubiquitous 10-20-30 rule was first introduced by Guy Kawasaki (entrepreneurial author and speaker) that refers to three basic pitching rules: you should have no more than 10 slides, your pitch is never more than 20 minutes, and never use smaller than 30-point font in your slide deck.

If you have a physical prototype to show during your pitch, you can include a demonstration or pass it around to the judges, investors, and/or audience. But, like the video slides, make sure it works beforehand, and practice your demonstration just as you do your pitch. The only downside of featuring your physical prototype is that any time you use a prop, you risk distracting the audience from your message. Use props only when necessary.

Appearance and Body Language

As part of your preparation, take time to attend to your appearance and mannerisms and how those relate to what you are selling. Match your appearance to the level of conservatism of your product or service. For example, if you've created a luxury line of perfume or clothing and expect to appeal to high-end clients, then present yourself in an attractive and sophisticated manner by wearing a designer suit and designer shoes. On the other hand, if you are selling geeky technology, you might consider an understated hipster style, and if you're selling surf-related items, dress in casual business, or even brand-related, clothing.

Concerning grooming, your nails should be manicured, your face trimmed (if you're a guy) and your hair presented in a sleek, trendy style. If you're a woman, learn to make up your face professionally. You can do this for free at a department store. It is critical that you brand yourself in a manner that complements your product or service. "You" have to make sense to the audience in order to be a believable creator and seller of the product.

Though it may sound strange, body language goes a long way in convincing audiences — people actually judge you by it. As you pitch your product, pay attention to your body language. Pitching skills aren't just about what you say. You must recognize that your audience is taking in the whole picture, including how you are dressed and how you move. Consciously or subconsciously, they are sizing up the brand of "you" and investing in you as much as they are the concept you are presenting.

In general, don't worry about what every gesture or body posture could mean. Simply make sure you are not doing anything distracting or annoying. We had a student who always held a pen in his hand whenever he pitched. He would click it to open and click it to close over and over. Imagine: Click! Click! Click! The sound was so distracting that it was hard to listen to him, and his fidgeting made him appear unpolished. We stopped him during his practice pitch and asked him to put the pen down. Curiously, he had no idea it was in his hand. Don't hold anything in your hand except a slide clicker, if you are presenting with slides.

As part of your body language, make sure your facial expressions are congruent with what you're saying, and smile during your presentation. Listeners want to know that you are open, friendly, enthusiastic, confident, and intelligent. Smiling and articulating with a degree of excitement exudes confidence.

Tone of voice also goes a long way in persuading people. Monitor your voice articulation, and modulate your tone. If you speak too softly, not only will people struggle to hear you, but also it will convey a lack of confidence. Strive to speak with enthusiasm, a little louder than you would normally speak.

Like our pen-clicking student, most people aren't aware of subtle body language or tone of voice, so once you have your pitch down, videotape yourself. You will be amazed at the details you notice while watching yourself that you don't notice while presenting. Critique yourself by applying the above factors on tone of voice and body language, and see what you can improve upon. Then practice more — again and again. Finally, practice your pitch in front of friends and mentors who will be brutally honest with you.

Research: We suggest spending at least 4 hours practicing your prepared pitch — practice a minimum of 20 times before you actually present.

Prepare Answers to Tough Questions

As part of your preparation, practice answering tough business and financial questions. Play devil's advocate, and list as many objections to your product idea as you can. Then practice answering each objection so your response sounds factual, convincing, and not defensive. Recognize that an objection by an investor or judge is an opportunity to sell, so there's no reason to overreact in an adversarial manner. An objection often signals that the investor is very interested. Know your numbers and your manufacturing process, and confidently convey them. If someone asks a question you don't know the answer to, be honest and tell him or her you will research the answer. Remember: The investors are buying into your product idea, and, more importantly, they are buying "you."

Connect with Judges

Once you walk into the competition or event and it's time for you to pitch, before you say a word, make eye contact with the judges, firmly shake hands, and confidently introduce yourself. This is also the time to distribute your card, marketing materials, and/or prototype. Show your passion, excitement and enthusiasm! Pump yourself up, and go for it!

When you finish one event, move onto the next. It's why we say, "pitch, pitch, and pitch again!" Enter as many competitions and pitch events as you can, whenever and wherever. Your goal is to win. But whether you win, place or show, the key is to develop recognition. Even if the rewards are small, you can claim to have developed an award-winning product.

Kevin Nguyen (center front glasses) and team

There is no other way to securing investment than pitching. This company solves a pain for entrepreneurs and helps create that desperately needed "amazing" presentation.

The Founders

Kenny Nguyen was a sophomore in Business Accounting at Louisiana State University and the president/founder of the student entrepreneur organization called "I am Entrepreneur." He graduated in 2009 from St. Michael High School and while there started the Cooking Club, an organization where students learned how to make simple quick dishes at home.

Gus Murillo was a freshman in Biological Sciences at Louisiana State University and was an officer of the student entrepreneur organization with Kenny. He graduated in 2010 summa cum laude from the Dunham School and while there was involved in a jazz band.

Mission Statement > Our original mission statement and mantra is "Turning Presentations into Experiences."

Company Growth > A large part of our rapid growth is due to us promoting the ideology of our services, rather than just promoting our services themselves. We know that stopping the "Death by PowerPoint" trend is a much talked about subject that piques professionals' interests. So we focused on pushing out original content detailing our strategies on how one can stop bad presentations. This resulted in us being requested to speak at conferences, contribute to large media outlets, and being frequently mentioned in professional organizations.

Business Model > At Big Fish Presentations we help companies deliver experiences with their stories and ideas through three services: presentation design, presentation consulting/workshops, and commercial video production.

20
Plan the Exit

Our overarching start-up strategy is to create something new, validate the product concept through customers and actual sales, and then find another company that is bigger and better at ramping it up so that you can ultimately sell your business. In this step, we show you how to plan your exit early.

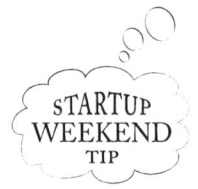

> **STARTUP WEEKEND TIP**
>
> THE BEST POSSIBLE OUTCOME FOR YOUR START-UP COULD BE TO SELL TO A BIGGER COMPANY. TRY DEVELOPING YOUR IDEA FROM THE BEGINNING WITH A SPECIFIC COMPANY IN MIND AS YOUR ENDGAME.

Many start-up "artists" are spectacular at starting something from nothing, but they are terrible at managing the long-term business. Think of the business world as populated by hunters and farmers. The hunters excel at start-ups, and the farmers are great at running the company long term. It is important to recognize your limitations from the outset. Very few people are both excellent hunters and farmers.

Take stock of what you are good at doing day-to-day. In so doing, consider not only what you like doing every day, but also what you are really effective at day-to-day. For example, do you excel at managing long-term projects, or do you get bored after you set up the infrastructure and strategic plan? Do you tend to fall in love with your creations and resist letting them go, or are you happy turning them over and trusting someone else to do a better job? Are you comfortable with the thought of managing more than 25 employees, or would you rather work with a start-up team and let someone else take care of hiring and managing? Do you get along with everyone and offer support to those around you, or would you rather leave that to someone else?

Once you've reviewed your strengths and weaknesses, identify realistic companies for your acquisition plan. Some entrepreneurs plan their products around a large company from the beginning. In fact, the founders of Barefoot Wine did this. They targeted Gallo from the beginning and built a brand they knew would attract Gallo. It worked — eventually. It took 20 years to build a brand attractive enough for such a large buyer. We want your exit to take place within 2 to 3 years of inception.

In order to do so, select companies that already sell similar, but not necessarily competitive, products. Some questions to ask yourself are: Does your product target a different gender or age group? Could it have a different application? Would it be sold through the same distribution system? And, could it be sold to the current customers of the target company?

Select companies you believe need your product or would want to buy it in order to either develop it, or to shore-up the potential competitive threat your business poses. Select companies that already have distribution channels for their other products. Ideal companies to target for your exit would sell through the same or similar distribution system as you would. If your product requires manufacturing, select companies that are proven manufacturers. Retailers are often gun-shy of new and unproven manufacturers. Developing well-connected, credible retailers' trust is critical for your future exit strategy.

Acquisition

There are several scenarios to consider as you plan your exit strategy, including acquisition, licensing deals, and earn-out.

In terms of acquisition, identify what company, or companies, might simply buy-out your product once you prove it is successful. Business valuation of a privately held company is a complicated subject involving analysis of economic conditions, financial statements, net present values, and securities. But to obtain a rough idea of your company's worth, employ a simple market approach using a valuation multiple. The number you use for a multiple depends on the recent activity in the market and the value of other companies in your industry. An easy way is to multiply your net sales by a number. This number, known as a multiplier, fluctuates greatly between industries and can range anywhere from 2 to 20. A very rough rule of thumb is to use anywhere from 3 to 10 as a multiplier. Generally, high-tech company multipliers are higher. If you know the multiplier commonly used in your industry, you can roughly estimate the value of your company based on your annual net sales. There are valuation experts that can help you determine a realistic value based on multipliers and other factors, such as recent acquisitions. However, keep in mind that until you are selling products at full capacity, your gross revenues will not reflect the full earning potential, so there is room for negotiation. Some businesses are still in the research and development (R & D) phase when they begin to raise funds and have no revenues at all — but can sell their company for relatively high values based alone on *potential* revenue.

Licensing

Licensing can also be stated as part of your business model, as opposed to an exit strategy. Typically the entrepreneur stays in business, and a license can become a separate asset. The value of this license can be incorporated into a negotiated acquisition price.

With a licensing deal, you continue to own the product and the patents. You may consider different options, such as an exclusive license with

I KNOW WE CAN SUCCESSFULLY GROW OUR COMPANY IN THE FIRST 24 MONTHS, BUT WE DON'T HAVE THE CAPITAL OR THE MANAGEMENT SKILLS TO HANDLE MORE THAN 20 EMPLOYEES
Sales are up!
WHAT DO YOU SUGGEST?"

BIG COMPANIES HAVE THE INFRASTRUCTURE IN PLACE WHO CAN OPERATE BIGGER BUSINESS UNITS. WHO MIGHT BUY US IN THE FUTURE?
HERE ARE THREE LARGE COMPANIES THAT HAVE PRODUCT LINES SYNERGISTIC TO OURS
potential exit strategies
BUT WE ARE DOING SO WELL, AND THIS IS OUR BABY! I DON'T WANT TO SELL

one company or a non-exclusive with many. If the licensing company does not meet your expectations, you can terminate the relationship and license with another company. However, keep in mind that an exclusive license precludes the inventors from using the invention or developing another product using their patent. You can negotiate a variation on the exclusive license where you reserve the right to practice the invention. This way, if the licensee fails to perform, you can avoid a protracted lawsuit to recover your invention.

Earn-Out

In an earn-out deal, a firm pays you cash up-front, but you are contractually obligated to stay with the company during its transition period. This is very common for acquisitions, whereby the acquiring firm desires to keep the original leaders onboard during a transitional period. Your "earn out" equals a percentage of the company's sale of your product — often as much as 30% of gross revenues of your product sales. Earn-out deals can also be based on duration with the acquired entity.

We have seen mixed results — and desires — regarding exit strategies, based on our students' experiences. Some want to run with their product into the distant future, and others desire a quick exit. Sometimes, the exit doesn't exist right around the corner, so they must either give up or stick with the product until a buyer comes along. The longer entrepreneurs work with their products or companies, the more attached they often get to them, and emotions can influence key decision when an exit opportunity arises. Staying objective is mandatory.

In summary, here are a few key exit lessons:
1. A buyer comes along when you least expect it. That *always* warrants serious consideration and is usually the time to sell.
2. The best time to sell is when you're making a lot of money and you feel the least urgency to sell. It's called "selling on a high."
3. By contrast, the worst time to sell is when you're running out of money and have a "fire sale," selling way below your company's potential worth. In this scenario, the buyer wins, and you lose.

Your company attracts buyers for a reason: The sales are flowing, and you are making more money than you ever thought possible. You are living the high life and clinking champagne glasses! You finally see the fruits of potentially 2 or 3 years of sweat equity. A buyer comes along with a great offer, and your knee jerk reaction is, "No way! This is my baby!" As counterintuitive as it may seem, in the moment, this is the best time to sell.

Without major help, your chances of long-term continued success are pretty low. You've never run a big company before, and a potential buyer knows exactly what to do next — and possesses the capital and human resources to execute a winning strategy. Statistics show your chances of failure in the next 3 years are pretty high. You need to swallow your pride and make your first really big business decision. Our advice is to sell it, take the money, and start something new.

NOTES

MORE REVIEWS

Simple, straightforward and practical information.

John Stump, President
StumpCo, Inc. Design & Engineering

• •

An incredible amount of information presented in an easy to process, succinct format. I will most certainly refer to this book when I start my next business venture.

Joseph R. Halsell, President
Halsell Builders, Inc.

The author is a true genius in starting your own company. The information contained in this book is invaluable. A must read for anyone wanting to start their own company.

Michelle Snyder Dettelis, CFO
Dance Motions, Inc.

A clear and stepwise approach to starting a business. A must read for every enthusiastic entrepreneur in the making.

Jay Jeths, Managing Director
Calyx, B.V. Netherlands

Simple, straightforward and practical information for any entrepreneur wannabe.

Chris Summers, President
VIP Pools, Inc.

This book provides detailed steps for acting on an idea and quickly starting a business. The author is so painfully correct when she says, 'You can't make money while sitting in the classroom.' I wish someone would have told me that when I was still in college.

Archie Mitchell, CEO
Pacific Coast Honey, LLC

More Reviews

On the following pages, you will meet some of our students who participated in the Enterprise Launch program at the Scheinfeld Center for Entrepreneurship & Innovation at Santa Barbara City College. Each student helped to create a product or service and the majority made their first sales, all within a single semester. There are many more like them from the past, and in our future! If they can do it, so can you.

- Melissa Visconti Moreno

Justin Connell

Justin Connell, posing above with one of his original prototypes, says: *Melissa has embodied the American entrepreneurial spirit in her work with SBCC's Scheinfeld Center for Entrepreneurship and Innovation, and in doing so she has passed that spirit onto the students involved in its programs. A perfect example is when I came to SBCC. I was a full-time student athlete playing basketball. I was always interested in business, but I never thought I could start my own business until after college, once I had earned a degree. After hearing Melissa come to speak to my Intro to Business class, I decided to join her Enterprise Launch program, and the rest is history.*

The Problem> Justin discovered the problem of older people unable to continue their love of gardening because getting down on the ground and getting back up was too difficult.

The Solution> Garden on Wheelz™ is a raised mobile gardening bed to enable stand-up gardening. Justin currently runs his $2 million company.

Cindy Gutierrez

I have taken a lot of courses in my lifetime, but none have more altered my life than the 20-steps needed to launch your own company, as described in Melissa's book. I followed all the advice closely, and in the end, I won the $1,000 prize for the best business plan and the most likely to succeed company. That is a lot of money, especially when I received it in $1 bills. Now, I have my company up and operating. It's amazing how practical this experience has been.

The Problem> As a person that knows the challenges of physical therapy first hand, Cindy was aware of how abrasive braces can be on a person's skin during recovery from a major sprain of a body part, like the back, arm, or leg.

The Solution> Cindy is a seamstress and owns equipment to sew things professionally. She invented the double-layered sleeve to be placed on the body under the brace, effectively ending the chafing and irritation that occurs when using soft braces. She calls her product "Embrace™".

Lynn Hartell

I wholeheartedly endorse Melissa Moreno's approach to starting a business. It gave me the structure, encouragement and confidence to move forward on an idea that I have had for years. Her system helped me recognize criteria for a successful business, focus my attention and follow through with action. Many thanks, Melissa!

The Problem> Lynn, a Doctor of Physical Therapy, knows many people recovering from illness or injury do the wrong exercises that may, in many cases, actually worsen the condition rather than help.

The Solution> Lynn has practiced physical therapy through exercise for years, and she developed a unique method that focused exercise on specific parts of the body and specific musculature. Lynn used the course to launch her proprietary training method, Remedy Fitness™, and won Honorable Mention in the collegiate tier of the 2013 Scheinfeld Center New Venture Challenge.

I joined the Fertile Grounds™ team at Santa Barbara City College, pitched the concept at the Scheinfeld Center New Venture Challenge and won First Place! Since then I have run with this concept using the $4,500 in seed capital won at the Challenge and created my own company with another student partner. One of the most valuable steps that I learned from the 20 Step process was how to pitch to win.

The Problem> As part of the new breed of eco-capitalist, Paulo was part of a team that tackled the problem of a billion pounds of waste in the form of used coffee grounds produced annually.

The Solution> Paulo and the team created a waste-based business collecting "scrap" coffee grounds, and processing them into both dry and liquid fertilizer, which his team sells to local farmers and home gardeners.

Robert & Dan

Dan says: *Santa Barbara City College's Enterprise Launch effectively changed my life. Enterprise Launch transformed me from a child with no sense of direction to a passionate and driven entrepreneur with goals, dreams and all of the tools needed to be successful in the fast-paced business world.*

The Problem> Robert Herr and Dan Friedman were original participants in our pilot course. They saw the problem of not being able to easily charge your phone, especially on the go.

The Solution> Their business, FuelBox™, revolutionizes the way we charge our phones. Their idea was somewhat discouraged, as too big of a project for the semester. Despite our discouragement, they proceeded in class with our mentorship and created a prototype! They are now housed in our local Santa Barbara incubator, Synergy, and are working on research & development, final iterations with an imminent launch. Stay tuned!

Alfred & Ricardo (with Dr. Jon Anton)

Ricardo says: *Working with Jon and Melissa not only made me a go-getter, but they also helped me achieve my goals and aspirations. Melissa and Jon are an outstanding duo when it comes to mentoring striving entrepreneurs. The course contained a set of easy-to-follow guidelines that get engrained in your head once you work with them, but ideas from other students are all accepted warmly, and everyone feels welcome to share their thoughts. That makes for a good working environment that leads to great success!.*

The Problem> Alfred Pacheco and Ricardo Haynes saw the need for purchasers on Craigslist who need help with delivery of large items.

The Solution> CraigFetch™! CraigFetch is a convenient delivery service for purchasers and sellers on Craigslist. Their tag line is "We fetch so you don't have to." Their numerous sales during the semester distracted them from their schoolwork! This team won a $1,000 in Enterprise Launch Demo Day and placed second at the Scheinfeld Center New Venture Challenge.

Lauren Karml

There is something so special about taking a course like Melissa's; it is so applicable and inspiring. Melissa's course taught me that it is one thing to have a good idea or concept and another thing to make that idea profitable. The specific steps she outlines in her course are precise and valuable. Melissa's course truly changed the way I look at the world and how I view business and entrepreneurship.

The Problem> As part of the new breed of eco-capitalist, Lauren was part of a team that tackled the problem of a billion pounds of waste in the form of used coffee grounds produced annually.

The Solution> Lauren and the team created a waste-based business which collects "scrap" coffee grounds and processes them into both dry and liquid fertilizer. Then her team sells the fertilizer to local farmers and home gardeners. The business is called Fertile Grounds™.

Melissa has the rare gift for removing the fog that so often cloud s the dreamer from the goal by teaching effective, specific methods to achieve the result. By the end your business plan is completely thought out and you are ready to go! Thanks for the great class. I will always remember it :) .

The Problem> Josef observed the problem of ineffective yet expensive skin care products, especially moisturizers.

The Solution> Josef invented his own moisturizer containing special oils imported from regions in Africa. He also created his own brand "Josef" with very attractive, elegant and eco-friendly packaging. Everyone loved Josef's product. Before the end of the semester he landed placement in a high-end hotel salon in Santa Barbara.

Mats Myhre

I gained tremendous and very valuable experience from the steps of launching my own business. The Enterprise Launch course was really a game changer for me. Melissa is both a great mentor that really knows how to motivate and push the students to success. During the course I learned by doing. The class really gives you hands on experience and the opportunity to take your dreams to reality. It's by far one of the most important courses I have taken on my journey to become a true entrepreneur.

The Problem> Mats has a hobby of wood working and carpentry. He is also a naturalist and hates to see people throwing so much furniture away that can be repurposed, thereby hurting the environment.

The Solution> Mats applied his wood working skills to repurpose and restore old wood furniture. He was amazed that he could acquire these old "gems" for almost free, then turn around and sell them at a profit after he applied his skills. His company is called AquaTree Restoration™.

Matt Shellnut

While at Santa Barbara City College, I took the Enterprise Launch course taught by Melissa Moreno. I knew very little about business at the time but thought it would be a good supplement to my education. This course ended up being one of the most useful I have ever taken because of how readily applicable it is. The 20 steps are very practical and made it easy to get my company started. I would recommend this book and course to anyone who has ever thought of starting their own business, and even to those who haven't. We're all just one idea away from a new business.

The Problem> Matt and his family are into grilling meat on the open fire. He realized that most meat sauces used during cooking are applied to the surface, fall into the fire and fail to season the meat

The Solution> Matt's solution was both simple and elegant. With the help of his grandfather, Matt manufactured a high-grade stainless steel injector called The Adder™ (patent pending) with which you can inject both solids (like chopped garlic and basil) and sauces into a thick piece of meat for the perfect flavor. He began selling the kitchen tool before the end of the semester. Brilliant!

Caleb Michael

I took Melissa's Enterprise Launch course while attending Santa Barbara City College. I went from not knowing anything about a business plan, to being able to confidently present my product to a panel of judges with success. It was definitely the most useful program I have taken at the school. The experience took the mystery out of starting a business and helped me discover a passion I will pursue for the rest of my life.

The Problem> As part of the new breed of eco-capitalist, Caleb was part of a team that tackled the problem of a billion pounds of waste in the form of used coffee grounds produced annually.

The Solution> Caleb and the team created a waste-based business collecting "scrap" coffee grounds, and processing them into both dry and liquid fertilizer which his team sells to local farmers and home gardeners. The business is called Fertile Grounds™.

Jack Weinstein

Taking the Enterprise Launch course offered at Santa Barbara City College has been one of my best decisions yet. The course provides students with all of the resources needed in starting up a business. Melissa immerses herself into each student product as if it is her own. I highly recommend this program to any student looking to start up his or her own company, or just to students with some entrepreneurial drive.

The Problem> Jack, like many students in Santa Barbara, had his bicycle stolen several times, even when locked — so he carries his bike upstairs to his apartment several times a day, which causes shoulder pain.

The Solution> Jack used his common sense to design a simple add-on for all bikes that makes it really easy and comfortable to place the bike on your shoulder and carry it up the stairs to your apartment or patio. His first prototype was a hand-drawing on a piece of paper to make it easier for him to share the product concept with others. He then employed a CAD engineer to digitally create the product and used Home Depot materials to build a prototype.

Donald Perkins

I took Melissa Moreno's Enterprise Launch course while attending Santa Barbara City College. This was one of the most useful courses that I have ever taken, and it definitely helped me prepare to launch my company. The 20 steps are specific and actionable and took the mystery out of starting a business. I recommend the course and her book.

The Problem> When business travelers visit a city with which they are not very familiar, the challenge often is what to do at night after work.

The Solution> Don created a smart phone App that helps the visiting business executive find entertainment, places to eat, and what to do for relaxation when in a strange city.

Joe Strong

The Enterprise Launch course taught by Melissa Moreno was a huge help when I needed to start the patent process for my product. Every classroom mentor is very knowledgeable in their field. This course makes it so you do not have to learn the hard way in so many new situations when starting up a business.

The Problem> Joe noticed that students who smoke use butane lighters, and inhale unhealthy noxious fumes.

The Solution> Joe's invention was a hemp wick lighter that minimized the use of the butane, employing a hemp wick to maximize the use of a single flame. Joe sold hundreds of these hemp lighters during the semester to retailers up and down the State of California and his business continues to expand.

Joel Angeles

Starting a company is like a roller coaster ride with tremendous sharp turns, sudden drops, and stops. Becoming an entrepreneur is no longer that impossible dream when I was given the opportunity to work with great minds. Melissa has transformed the 'impossible' that kept me from being a successful entrepreneur. She helped me believe in myself and see that "I'm possible" in anything I put my mind to.

The Problem> Joel is very interested in educating the younger generation. He found that most schools do not have the tools that really ignite student interest and curiosity.

The Solution> Joel invented the Smart Finger Puppet™, an adorable knit finger sleeve that looks like an historical figure (e.g., Einstein, Hans Christian Anderson, Isaac Newton) with a capacitor for a touch screen that allows young students to wear the puppet while navigating and researching the character on a touch screen. He is now manufacturing overseas and selling.

Johnny Olaguez

We all start in the same place and, believe it or not, with the same resources. It's up to you to come up with a recipe that makes the magic happen.

The Problem> Johnny is obsessed with water conservation and is concerned about the water that is wasted while taking a shower and soaping up.

The Solution> Johnny came up with a shower "shut-off" valve that could easily stop the supply to the shower head without having to re-set the hot and cold water feed when you turned it back on. With the push of a button, the water shuts off and goes back on easily during your shower time, while keeping the perfect water temperature.

Ty Blunt

I always have known that I wanted to be an entrepreneur. But before I joined Enterprise Launch at SBCC, I was walking in the dark trying to find my way. After learning the multiple steps to launch my company, I am in full production and sales mode. With Melissa's help I have produced prototypes and am ready to start manufacturing the final prototype. I owe Melissa everything I have done so far with my product. The 20 Step process is the way to go.

The Problem> Women carry many different nail accessories in their purses to groom on the go (e.g., files, scissors, cuticle trimmers). These are bulky and expensive to buy individually.

The Solution> Ty invented what he called the NAK™. His product combines the nail grooming tools into one sleekly designed unit. It is light, and easy to store in a purse, and efficiently priced. During the Enterprise Launch program, he discovered a sales niche with trade show vendors for use as a vendor branded give-away.

The Enterprise Launch course at Santa Barbara City College transformed my dreams into very realistic goals. In only one semester, I went from complete ignorance in the business world, to having a firm understanding on how to launch a successful business! Melissa and Jon are wonderful and knowledgeable mentors.

The Problem> Many owners of large yachts look for talented interior designers to help them design a more comfortable and more unique interior of their dining room, master bedroom, and living room. There are very few, if any, individuals who offer such a service.

The Solution> Marissa and her partner are studying interior design at SBCC. During the semester, they started a company to provide a special service to owners of large yachts parked in the Santa Barbara Harbor. Their recommendations for a 30 foot sailing yacht at the Marina were submitted and adopted by the owner.

Appendix A
Matrix of Skills

Strengths	Weaknesses
• What skills or traits do you have that others don't have (talent, certificates, education, vocational training, connections, patience, people-person) • What do you do better than anyone else? • What personal resources can you access? (truck, lathe, machinery) • What do other people (your boss or professor) see as your strengths? • What achievements are you proud of? (sports, grades, family) • What values do you have that you see other people don't have? • Are you connected with influential people or networks?	• What tasks do you avoid because you don't feel confident? • What do other people see as your weaknesses? • Where are you weakest in your educational or vocational training? (math, science, people skills) • What are your negative work or study habits? (procrastinator, always late, disorganized, short-tempered) • Do you attempt to hide negative personality traits? (afraid of public speaking, shyness)
Opportunities • What new technology can help you? • What new skills are you acquiring at work or in school that will advance you or opportunities? • Can you get help from others or from people via the Internet? • Do you have a network of strategic contacts to help you, or offer good advice?	**Threats** • What obstacles do you face at work or school? • Does changing technology hold you back? • What personal issues do you have that will interrupt progress?

Appendix B1
Personality Self-Assessment

Step 1: Select the words in each column in the table below that you would use to describe yourself. Circle only those words that really describe you as you are today, not what you would like to be in the future. Be critical and select only those that are a near-perfect fit.

Type A	Type B	Type C	Type D
expressive	driver	amiable	analytic
articulate	likes to lead	good listener	likes numbers
outgoing	takes notes	mediator	introvert
good dresser	get-it-done type	thinks about feelings	considered smart
extravert	task oriented	is emotional	geek-like
pushy	charismatic	likes people	into details
center of attention	attracts followers	avoids conflict	guru type
Total Words Circled	**Total Words Circled**	**Total Words Circled**	**Total Words Circled**
#	#	#	#

Using the largest number at the bottom of each column, determine your Personality Type: A B C D.

Step 2. What is your primary area of career interest? Select the careers in each of the columns below. Circle only those careers that are a near-perfect fit for you.

Type A	Type B	Type C	Type D
marketing	business admin	English literature	engineering
theater - acting	law	music	medicine
public speaking	military science	financial planning	accounting
political science	management	human resources	mechanics
public office	government	social sciences	physics
sales	sport management	architecture	chemistry
TV commentator	international affairs	art appreciation	biology
Total Careers Circled	**Total Careers Circled**	**Total Careers Circled**	**Total Careers Circled**
#	#	#	#

Using the largest number at the bottom of each column, determine your Career Interests: A B C D

Step 3. Add the totals in each of the four columns in *both* of the tables above.

Total Type A: _____   Total Type B: _____   Total Type C: _____   Total Type D: _____

Type A	Type B	Type C	Type D
Expressive	Driver	Amiable	Analytic

Circle your strongest Type to end this Personality Self-Assessment

Appendix B2
Entrepreneur Self-Evaluation Table

Entrepreneur Self-Evaluation Table

15 Attributes Description	Your Score (0 – 10)	Weight (0-10)	Total (0 – 100)
1. Generous		04	
2. Detailed		05	
3. Courageous		06	
4. Crisis Proof		07	
5. Analytic		08	
6. Articulate		09	
7. Can Do		09	
8. Optimistic		10	
9. Passionate		10	
10. Creative		10	
11. Focused		10	
12. Persistent		10	
13. Honest		10	
14. Responsible		10	
15. High Risk		10	
Total			
			Maximum Score 1,280

Likelihood of Entrepreneurial Success

Your Score	25%	50%	75%	100%
	500	600	900	1,200

Appendix C1
Sample Partnership Agreement
(Source: Entrepreneur.com)

THIS PARTNERSHIP AGREEMENT is made this _____ day of _____, 20__, by and between the following individuals:

Name:_____
Address:_____
_____
_____

Name:_____
Address:_____
_____
_____

1. <u>Nature of Business</u>. The partners listed above hereby agree that they shall be considered partners in business for the following purpose:
_____

___
_____

___

2. <u>Name</u>. The partnership shall be conducted under the name of _____ and shall maintain offices at [STREET ADDRESS], [CITY, STATE, ZIP].

3. <u>Day-To-Day Operation</u>. The partners shall provide their full-time services and best efforts on behalf of the partnership. No partner shall receive a salary for services rendered to the partnership. Each partner shall have equal rights to manage and control the partnership and its business. Should there be differences between the partners concerning ordinary business matters, a decision shall be made by unanimous vote. It is understood that the partners may elect one of the partners to conduct the day-to-day business of the partnership; however, no partner shall be able to bind the partnership by act or contract to any liability exceeding $_____ without the prior written consent of each partner.

4. <u>Capital Contribution</u>. The capital contribution of each partner to the partnership shall consist of the following property, services, or cash which each partner agrees to contribute:

Name Of Partner	Capital Contribution	Agreed-Upon Cash	% Share

The partnership shall maintain a capital account record for each partner; should any partner's capital account fall below the agreed to amount, then that partner shall (1) have his share of partnership profits then due and payable applied instead to his capital account; and (2) pay any deficiency to the partnership if his share of partnership profits is not yet due and payable or, if it is, his share is insufficient to cancel the deficiency.

Appendix C2
Sample Partnership Agreement
(Source: Entrepreneur.com)

5. Profits and Losses. The profits and losses of the partnership shall be divided by the partners according to a mutually agreeable schedule and at the end of each calendar year according to the proportions listed above.

6. Term/Termination. The term of this Agreement shall be for a period of _____ years, unless the partners mutually agree in writing to a shorter period. Should the partnership be terminated by unanimous vote, the assets and cash of the partnership shall be used to pay all creditors, with the remaining amounts to be distributed to the partners according to their proportionate share.

7. Disputes. This Partnership Agreement shall be governed by the laws of the State of _____. Any disputes arising between the partners as a result of this Agreement shall be settled by arbitration in accordance with the rules of the American Arbitration Association and judgment upon the award rendered may be entered in any court having jurisdiction thereof.

8. Withdrawal/Death of Partner. In the event a partner withdraws or retires from the partnership for any reason, including death, the remaining partners may continue to operate the partnership using the same name. A withdrawing partner shall be obligated to give sixty (60) days' prior written notice of his/her intention to withdraw or retire and shall be obligated to sell his/her interest in the partnership. No partner shall transfer interest in the partnership to any other party without the written consent of the remaining partner(s). The remaining partner(s) shall pay the withdrawing or retiring partner, or to the legal representative of the deceased or disabled partner, the value of his interest in the partnership, or (a) the sum of his capital account, (b) any unpaid loans due him, (c) his proportionate share of accrued net profits remaining undistributed in his capital account, and (d) his interest in any prior agreed appreciation in the value of the partnership property over its book value. No value for good will shall be included in determining the value of the partner's interest.

9. Non-Compete Agreement. A partner who retires or withdraws from the partnership shall not directly or indirectly engage in a business which is or which would be competitive with the existing or then anticipated business of the partnership for a period of _____, in those _____ of this State where the partnership is currently doing or planning to do business.

IN WITNESS WHEREOF, the partners have duly executed this Agreement on the day and year set forth hereinabove.

_____   _____
Partner   Partner

Terms of Use
Please note: Prior to using these forms, please consult with an attorney or other expert knowledgeable in the laws of the applicable jurisdiction and the specific intended use of those forms.

All forms are general in nature; are not based on the laws of any specific state or other juridiction but rather general principles of law applicable throughout the United States; and should only be used after first consulting with an attorney or other expert knowledgeable in the laws of the applicable jurisdiction and the specific intended use of those forms.

Appendices

Appendix D1
Sample Nondisclosure Agreement
(Source: Nolo.com)

This Nondisclosure Agreement (the "Agreement") is entered into by and between _____ with its principal offices at _____ ("Disclosing Party") and _____, located at _____ ("Receiving Party") for the purpose of preventing the unauthorized disclosure of Confidential Information as defined below. The parties agree to enter into a confidential relationship with respect to the disclosure of certain proprietary and confidential information ("Confidential Information").

1. **Definition of Confidential Information.** For purposes of this Agreement, "Confidential Information" shall include all information or material that has or could have commercial value or other utility in the business in which Disclosing Party is engaged. If Confidential Information is in written form, the Disclosing Party shall label or stamp the materials with the word "Confidential" or some similar warning. If Confidential Information is transmitted orally, the Disclosing Party shall promptly provide a writing indicating that such oral communication constituted Confidential Information.

2. **Exclusions from Confidential Information.** Receiving Party's obligations under this Agreement do not extend to information that is: (a) publicly known at the time of disclosure or subsequently becomes publicly known through no fault of the Receiving Party; (b) discovered or created by the Receiving Party before disclosure by Disclosing Party; (c) learned by the Receiving Party through legitimate means other than from the Disclosing Party or Disclosing Party's representatives; or (d) is disclosed by Receiving Party with Disclosing Party's prior written approval.

3. **Obligations of Receiving Party.** Receiving Party shall hold and maintain the Confidential Information in strictest confidence for the sole and exclusive benefit of the Disclosing Party. Receiving Party shall carefully restrict access to Confidential Information to employees, contractors, and third parties as is reasonably required and shall require those persons to sign nondisclosure restrictions at least as protective as those in this Agreement. Receiving Party shall not, without prior written approval of Disclosing Party, use for Receiving Party's own benefit, publish, copy, or otherwise disclose to others, or permit the use by others for their benefit or to the detriment of Disclosing Party, any Confidential Information. Receiving Party shall return to Disclosing Party any and all records, notes, and other written, printed, or tangible materials in its possession pertaining to Confidential Information immediately if Disclosing Party requests it in writing.

4. **Time Periods.** The nondisclosure provisions of this Agreement shall survive the termination of this Agreement and Receiving Party's duty to hold Confidential Information in confidence shall remain in effect until the Confidential Information no longer qualifies as a trade secret or until Disclosing Party sends Receiving

Appendix D2
Sample Nondisclosure Agreement
(Source: Nolo.com)

Party written notice releasing Receiving Party from this Agreement, whichever occurs first.

5. **Relationships.** Nothing contained in this Agreement shall be deemed to constitute either party a partner, joint venturer or employee of the other party for any purpose.

6. **Severability.** If a court finds any provision of this Agreement invalid or unenforceable, the remainder of this Agreement shall be interpreted so as best to effect the intent of the parties.

7. **Integration.** This Agreement expresses the complete understanding of the parties with respect to the subject matter and supersedes all prior proposals, agreements, representations, and understandings. This Agreement may not be amended except in a writing signed by both parties.

8. **Waiver.** The failure to exercise any right provided in this Agreement shall not be a waiver of prior or subsequent rights.
This Agreement and each party's obligations shall be binding on the representatives, assigns, and successors of such party. Each party has signed this Agreement through its authorized representative.

Disclosing Party
By: _____
Printed Name: _____
Title: _____
Dated: _____

Receiving Party
By: _____
Printed Name: _____
Title: _____
Dated: _____

Terms of Use
Please note: Prior to using these forms, please consult with an attorney or other expert knowledgeable in the laws of the applicable jurisdiction and the specific intended use of those forms.

All forms are general in nature, are not based on the laws of any specific state or other juridiction but rather general principles of law applicable throughout the United States; and should only be used after first consulting with an attorney or other expert knowledgeable in the laws of the applicable jurisdiction and the specific intended use of those forms.

Appendix E1
Sample Financial Template

Your Company's Financial Model	1	2	3	4	5	6	TOTALS
(First six months)							
Non-recurring Expenses							
Build a Prototype							
Create a Website							
Other (add more rows)							
Fixed Expenses							
Office Rental							
Insurance							
Legal Advice							
Accounting Advice							
Marketing							
Website Maintenance							
Your Survival Pay Check							
Other (add more rows)							
Sub-Total							
Variable Expenses							
Number of Units Built							
Cost per Unit Built							
Number of Units Sold							
Price per Unit Sold							
Shipping (if any)							
Travel Expenses							
Product Brochures							
Other (add more rows)							
Sub-Total							
Fixed plus Variable Expenses							
Total Revenue							
Monthly Income or Loss							
Cumulative Income or Loss							

Appendix E2
Sample Financial Template

Your Company's Financial Model	7	8	9	10	11	12	TOTALS
(Second six months)							
Non-recurring Expenses							
Build a Prototype							
Create a Website							
Other (add more rows)							
Fixed Expenses							
Office Rental							
Insurance							
Legal Advice							
Accounting Advice							
Marketing							
Website Maintenance							
Your Survival Pay Check							
Other (add more rows)							
Sub-Total							
Variable Expenses							
Number of Units Built							
Cost per Unit Built							
Number of Units Sold							
Price per Unit Sold							
Shipping (if any)							
Travel Expenses							
Product Brochures							
Other (add more rows)							
Sub-Total							
Fixed plus Variable Expenses							
Total Revenue							
Monthly Income or Loss							
Cumulative Income or Loss							

Appendix F
Sample Cash Flow Forecast

Sample Data for Discussion Only

Your Company™							
Months after Launch	1	2	3	4	5	6	TOTALS
Fixed Expenses							
Manufacturing and Office Rental	$300	$300	$300	$300	$300	$300	$1,800
Product Liability Insurance	$75	$75	$75	$75	$75	$75	$450
Legal Advice	$50	$50	$50	$50	$50	$50	$300
Accounting Advice	$25	$25	$25	$25	$25	$25	$150
Marketing	$20	$20	$20	$20	$20	$20	$120
Website Maintenance	$50	$50	$50	$50	$50	$50	$300
My Survival Pay	$1,000	$1,000	$1,000	$1,000	$1,000	$1,000	$6,000
Sub-Total	$1,520	$1,520	$1,520	$1,520	$1,520	$1,520	$9,120
Variable Expenses							
Number of Units Built	10	20	30	30	30	40	160
Cost per Unit Built	$75	$75	$75	$75	$75	$75	
Total Manufacturing Cost	$750	$1,500	$2,250	$2,250	$2,250	$3,000	$12,000
Number of Units Sold	5	20	25	30	35	40	155
Price per Unit Sold	$250	$250	$250	$250	$250	$250	
Nursery Commission	$188	$750	$938	$1,125	$1,313	$1,500	$5,813
Shipping (if any)	$50	$200	$250	$300	$350	$400	$1,550
Travel Expenses	$25	$100	$125	$150	$175	$200	$775
Product Brochures	$10	$40	$50	$60	$70	$80	$310
Sub-Total	$1,363	$2,955	$3,993	$4,270	$4,548	$5,585	$22,713
Fixed plus Variable Expenses	$2,883	$4,475	$5,513	$5,790	$6,068	$7,105	$31,833
Total Revenue	$1,250	$5,000	$6,250	$7,500	$8,750	$10,000	$38,750
Profit Margin	43.37%	111.73%	113.38%	129.53%	144.21%	140.75%	113.83%
Monthly Income or Loss	-$1,633	$525	$738	$1,710	$2,683	$2,895	$6,918
Cumulative Income or Loss	-$1,633	-$1,108	-$370	$1,340	$4,023	$6,918	
Inventory	5	5	10	10	5	5	

In the table above the reader can observe the big picture of all the numbers for the first six months.

Monthly Income or Loss	-$1,633	$525	$738	$1,710	$2,683	$2,895	$6,918
Cumulative Income or Loss	-$1,633	-$1,108	-$370	$1,340	$4,023	$6,918	

In the last two rows taken from the table above, the reader can observe the actual cash flow forecast for the first six months.

NOTES

Dr. Jon Anton
Subject Matter Expert

Dr. Jon Anton has made his career as a serial entrepreneur starting companies, growing them to about 30 employees, and then selling them to large public companies for a combination of cash and stock. He started 19 companies of which 12 failed miserably, 4 did pretty well, and 3 were proverbial "home runs," thereby, attaining a batting average of about .368!

Dr. Jon's formal education was in technology, including a Doctorate of Science and a Master of Science from Harvard University, a Master of Science from the University of Connecticut, and a Bachelor of Science from the University of Notre Dame. He also completed an intensive executive education program in Business at the Graduate School of Business at Stanford University.

Dr. Jon has authored 27 books on high-tech subjects, and is a frequent writer in professional and trade journals in his field.

He is currently the "entrepreneur-in-residence" for the Enterprise Launch program at Santa Barbara City College in California.

Dr. Melissa Visconti Moreno is Dean of Educational Programs at Santa Barbara City College in California and the founding Executive Director of the Scheinfeld Center for Entrepreneurship & Innovation. Under Melissa's direction, the Scheinfeld Center earned national recognition for program excellence and was awarded two regional designations as the Small Business Development Center and the Center for International Trade Development.

Melissa was born with a passion for teaching and continues to teach students in entrepreneurship. Her core philosophy for young entrepreneurs is *spend more time doing* and believes the two-year college setting is the perfect venue in which to kick-start entrepreneurs.

Melissa exercises her own entrepreneur muscle working on her new independent hotel brand and proprietary management system for independent hotel owners. For the past 20 years, as owner and CEO, she has run an independent hotel company in Arizona and Montana. She also consults for small businesses and start-ups.

**Melissa Visconti Moreno, J.D.
Author**

Melissa completed her undergraduate studies at University of California, Santa Barbara, and received her Juris Doctorate from the College of Law in Santa Barbara. She is admitted to the California State Bar and is a licensed California Real Estate Broker.